W9-ADQ-469

ISSUES THAT CONCERN YOU

Choosing a Career

Other books in the Issues That Concern You series:

$39.95

ISSUES THAT CONCERN YOU

Choosing a Career

Linda Aksomitis, *Book Editor*

GREENHAVEN PRESS
A part of Gale, Cengage Learning

GALE
CENGAGE Learning

Detroit • New York • San Francisco • New Haven, Conn • Waterville, Maine • London

DISCARDED

Shelton State Libraries
Shelton State Community College

Christine Nasso, Publisher
Elizabeth Des Chenes, Managing Editor

© 2009 Greenhaven Press, a part of Gale, Cengage Learning

Gale and Greenhaven Press are registered trademarks used herein under license.

For more information, contact:
Greenhaven Press
27500 Drake Rd.
Farmington Hills, MI 48331-3535
Or you can visit our Internet site at http://gale.cengage.com

ALL RIGHTS RESERVED.
No part of this work covered by the copyright herein may be reproduced, transmitted, stored, or used in any form or by any means graphic, electronic, or mechanical, including but not limited to photocopying, recording, scanning, digitizing, taping, Web distribution, information networks, or information storage and retrieval systems, except as permitted under Section 107 or 108 of the 1976 United States Copyright Act, without the prior written permission of the publisher.

For product information and technology assistance, contact us at

Gale Customer Support, 1-800-877-4253
For permission to use material from this text or product, submit all requests online at www.cengage.com/permissions

Further permissions questions can be emailed to permissionrequest@cengage.com

Articles in Greenhaven Press anthologies are often edited for length to meet page requirements. In addition, original titles of these works are changed to clearly present the main thesis and to explicitly indicate the author's opinion. Every effort is made to ensure that Greenhaven Press accurately reflects the original intent of the authors. Every effort has been made to trace the owners of copyrighted material.

Cover image © OJO Images/SuperStock

LIBRARY OF CONGRESS CATALOGING-IN-PUBLICATION DATA

Choosing a career / Linda Aksomitis, book editor.
      p. cm. — (Issues that concern you)
   Includes bibliographical references and index.
   ISBN-13: 978-0-7377-4184-1 (hardcover)
1. Career development. 2. Vocational guidance. 3. Educational counseling. I. Aksomitis, Linda.
   HF5381.C6545 2008
   331.702—dc22
                                                    2008021488

Printed in the United States of America
2 3 4 5 6 7 12 11 10 09 08

CONTENTS

Today, workers do not expect to spend a lifetime with a single employer as they may have in the 1950s or even the 1970s. The Bureau of Labor Statistics reports that the average person changes careers at least five times in a lifetime. In fact, the average American holds between ten and twelve jobs from school to retirement.

Teens preparing to enter the workforce need to put more planning into choosing a career than ever before, in order to prepare for a successful future. Choosing a career involves examining personal interests, abilities, and needs, and acquiring the skills and experience that will lead to job offers from employers.

Today, estimates suggest that between 20 percent and 50 percent of students entering college are undecided about their major. Those who have identified their major before beginning college coursework can begin preparing for a career right away. A student who has identified an interest in a communications career, for example, might enroll in a variety of courses such as technical writing, public speaking, and advertising. Upon graduation, that student has a broad skill set and is qualified to apply for a variety of different jobs.

In decades past, anyone who graduated from college with good grades could expect to quickly find a decent job in his or her field. Now, the job market is extremely competitive. Employers consider academic success, but they also look for indicators that applicants have been working toward a career for some time. Employers look for community service and volunteerism; leadership activities through school and community; and such preparation as career shadowing, internships, youth apprenticeships, and cooperative education.

While competition for good jobs may be fierce, some statistics indicate that the number of jobs is growing. The fall 2007

Today it is estimated that between 20 and 50 percent of students entering college are undecided about their major.

Occupational Quarterly from the U.S. Department of Labor, Bureau of Labor Statistics, projected that by 2016 there would be 166 million jobs in the United States. In 2006 there were only 151 million jobs. The types of jobs available to people continue to change as well.

In the coming years, the largest projected increases in employment will be in two sectors: service industries and professional and related areas. Each of these is predicted to have an increase of 17 percent. Jobs in service industries cover a wide range, including the restaurant and hotel industries, repairs, and personal care jobs. Professional and related occupations include such careers as computer programming, social work, health care, arts and entertainment, and architecture and engineering. Within this classification, computer and mathematical science occupations are projected to grow more than twice as fast as the average for all occupations.

Within each area of employment growth, however, the types of jobs and salary earning potential vary. Someone who prepares for a career in health care, for example, has many options depending on the type of training. The median annual salary in 2006 for a nursing aide, orderly, or attendant (for which the lowest qualification is high school graduation) was $19,420, while the median annual salary for a registered nurse (with two to four years' training) was $57,280.

Careers in the service industry often build on high school jobs, adding on-the-job and formal training for individuals who want

In 2006 thirteen of the top sixteen highest-paying jobs were in the health industry.

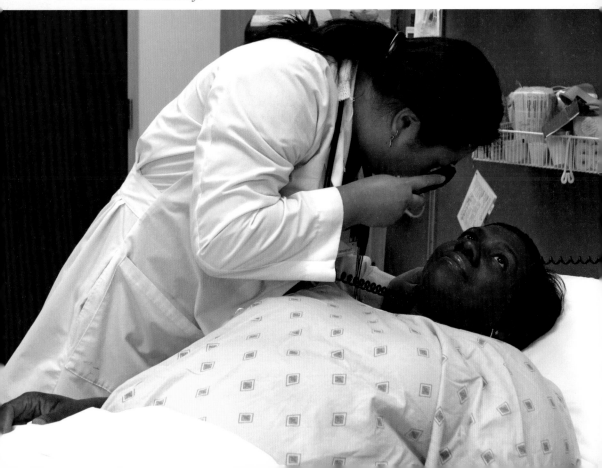

to change jobs or advance. While numerous jobs are available, earnings in the service industry are generally low. For example, the median annual salary of truck drivers, heavy and tractor-trailer, was $35,040 in 2006, while the median annual salary of food preparation and service workers (including fast food) was just $15,050.

Generally the highest-paying careers have several factors in common. Most high-paying jobs, for example, require extensive training and education. The degree of responsibility on the job is another factor in establishing wages—employees who are directly responsible for someone else's life, for instance, often earn higher salaries than those in jobs with lesser responsibilities. Responsibility on the job, however, comes in many forms. An employee may earn a higher salary because he or she is responsible for handling expensive equipment, like an earthmover for road construction. Those responsible for financial investments for a company or client also typically earn higher salaries.

In 2006, thirteen of the top sixteen highest-paying jobs were in the health industry, ranging from anesthesiologists at $145,600 annual median salary to podiatrists at $108,200. The non-health-care positions on the list were chief executives of corporations, airline pilots and flight engineers, and air traffic controllers.

Certainly, annual income is only one thing to consider when choosing a career. Successful career planning means thinking carefully about individual interests and how those interests can play a role in the workplace. It also requires developing a solid career path of education, work experience, community and extracurricular experience, and hobbies. There are many different ways to incorporate interests, skills, and passions into the workplace, and it is advisable to investigate the full range of career options.

The following viewpoints provide students with numerous perspectives on choosing a career. The authors of the viewpoints address the value of career planning, whether a college education can benefit all students, options available to students with disabilities, and the pursuit of nontraditional careers. In addition, the volume contains several appendixes to help the reader understand and explore career paths, including a thorough bibliography and a list of organizations to contact for further information. The appendix "What You Should Know About Choosing a Career" offers facts and statistics about education and careers in the United States, Canada, and elsewhere. The appendix "What You Should Do About Choosing a Career" offers tips to students that they can apply immediately to help them choose the career of their dreams.

ONE

Career Planning Is Important

Marilyn Harryman

In the following viewpoint Marilyn Harryman, the coordinator of counseling services in the Oakland Unified School District in California, states reasons why individuals should have a career plan. She asserts the importance of finding a career that is flexible, pays well, and is compatible with personal interests. Harryman points out that the ideal career fulfills a person's dreams and desires while also meeting practical needs.

What is a career life plan? This can be a difficult question, and requires careful thought. First, a career is a vocation. It is a lifetime endeavor for the purpose of growth and self-support. Your career, if well chosen, will follow you throughout your life and help to augment your understanding of the world and all of your experiences in life.

A Career Plan Allows for Many Different Jobs

You may have many jobs during your career life. In thinking about what you would like to do next, it is important to think about what career area interests you. Each career interest will more than likely offer you many different job opportunities. For instance, if you choose to work in education, your career may

Marilyn Harryman, "Career Life Plan," *EUREKA*, 2007. Reproduced by permission of the author.

span many jobs, such as teacher, education planner, counselor or school principal.

We live and we learn on a continuum. It is very difficult to divorce your career planning from the life you want to lead, because the two are completely interrelated. In thinking about what you would like to do next, it is important to think about what career area interests you as a person. A well-chosen career takes everything into account. Will you work during the day or night? How much will be your earning potential? How much flexibility will you have? A good career takes into account:

When making a career plan, one needs to take into account many factors, including work schedule, compensation, and job flexibility.

This information is taken from a survey of 2006 graduates of the bachelor of science in information management and technology degree program at Syracuse University in Syracuse, New York.

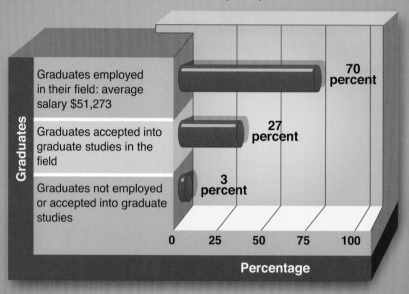

Taken from: School of Information Studies, "Career Planning: Student Success," Syracuse University, 2007. http://ischool.syr.edu/career/success.aspx.

- Work schedule
- Job flexibility
- Compensation
- Location
- Personal compatibility

. . . and many other considerations. Most importantly, the best career choice doesn't just include a few of these considerations, but all of them together.

A Career Plan Develops Personal Vision

Each of us is connected as a birthright and without any effort on our part to the life forces which flow through the world. Each of us has a connection to culture, to love, to energy, and to greatness. Regardless of the multitude of obstacles imposed by our circumstances, we can each prepare ourselves, in our own time, to have a profound impact on our own life, on our families, on our community, and on the world.

To build our connection to the positive universal forces, each of us must develop a vision for our life and for our future. Our vision does not lie outside of ourselves, but is already planted as a seed within us, waiting to blossom. In that vision is our passion, our courage, our hope and our opportunity for self-expression and fulfillment.

A Career Plan Unites Head and Heart

You may have heard the phrase "follow your heart, not your head." Yet, when you listen to your "heart," which is a way of describing the perspective of your inner person, your "head" may contradict your inner desires. The perspective in your "head"— your practical, logical side—will try to show you why your vision is impractical, won't work, and so forth. Yet, if you follow your "head," which many people do, you may spend many years regretting your choices, and hoping for an opportunity to "follow your heart."

The danger of allowing logic to rule over feelings is that logic is rooted in past experience. While our heart tugs us forward toward our vision, our head pulls us back to the reality of our current situation and our past experiences and limitations. Our head fashions these experiences into truths, and beliefs about ourselves, which limit our opportunities and anchor us in our current situation. Many people become so bound by their past, that they simply give up their vision. To hold on to our vision, we need to let go of limiting beliefs about ourselves and move forward.

To feel and be whole, you must take advantage of both your "heart" and your "head." . . . It's important to be both practical and idealistic when engaging in career planning . . . , to find what's in your "heart" and make it work with what's in your "head."

TWO

Career Planning Is a Waste of Time

Jeremy Dean

> Jeremy Dean asserts in the following viewpoint that career planning is a waste of time. He maintains that people often do not know what they want and have trouble predicting what they will want in the future, a concept described as "miswanting." Dean suggests that miswanting is the reason career planning is a painful process that yields little benefit. After obtaining a law degree and working as a writer, Dean pursued a master's degree in research methods in psychology at University College, London, England.

Our culture worships planning. Everything must be planned in advance. Our days, week, years, our entire lives. We have diaries, schedules, checklists, targets, goals, aims, strategies, visions even. Career planning is the most insidious of these cults precisely because it encourages a feeling of control over your reactions to future events. As that interview question goes: where do you see yourself in five years time? This invites the beginning of what starts as a little game and finishes as a belief built on sand. You guess what employers want to hear, and then you give it to them. Sometimes this batting back and forth of imagined futures becomes a necessary little game you play in order to 'get ahead'.

Jeremy Dean, "Why Career Planning Is Time Wasted," *PsyBlog*, March 21, 2007. Reproduced by permission.

The Number of Options Can Be Overwhelming

In reality, people frequently don't know what they want and psychology has proved it. That's why career planning, or at the very least just deciding what you're going to do next, is so unpleasant. It's no fun at 18 years old when people ask what you want to do. There seem to be so many different options, each with myriad branching possibilities, many of which lead in opposite directions, but all equally tempting. Surrounded by these endless spiralling futures, it is no wonder that many a school-leaver sticks with what they know and follows in parental footsteps. But we don't all want to trust the tried and tested, whether for good reasons or bad. We want to make a decision all of our own, based on our own values and preferences.

If it's hard at 18, it's even harder in midlife when people are theoretically better equipped to make their choice. In reality by your 30s wide-eyed optimism has normally been replaced by a

Career fairs are one way students can learn about jobs that may interest them.

©2003 Mike Keefe, the *Denver Post*, and PoliticalCartoon.com.

more cynical outlook on jobs and the workplace. Now it's more clear what the downsides of certain jobs are. There's not only our own experiences of work but we also have friends at work, all of whom colour our perception of their careers.

Career Planning Requires Predicting the Future

Everyone has their own internal trade-offs. How much routine do you like: boring but safe? How much do you like travel: exciting but you'll be away from loved ones? How much do you care about earning more money: and taking a more boring/stressful/less fulfilling job? Whatever the outcome of all these swings and roundabouts along with many more, the reason that deciding what to do with your life is so difficult is that it involves predicting the future.

There's many reasons why it seems we should be good at predicting what we want. If I know that I'm enjoying what I'm doing now, then I should enjoy it in the future, shouldn't I? On top of this I've got years of experience building up a set of things I like—cinema, books, sitcoms—and things I don't like—trips to the dentist, severe embarrassment and flu, especially not all at the same time. If I've got this huge bank of likes and dislikes it should be easy to predict my wants in the future. And yet, it seems we are often surprised by what the future throws at us.

People Are Poor at Predicting What Will Make Them Happy

The idea of making mistakes about what we might want in the future has been termed 'miswanting' by [O.T.] Gilbert and [T.D.] Wilson (2000). They point to a range of studies finding we are poor at predicting what will make us happy in the future. My favourite is a simple experiment in which two groups of participants get free sandwiches if they participate in the experiment—a doozie for any undergraduate.

One group has to choose which sandwiches they want for an entire week in advance. The other group gets to choose which they want each day. A fascinating thing happens. People who choose their favourite sandwich each day at lunchtime also often choose the same sandwich. This group turns out to be reasonably happy with its choice.

Amazingly, though, people choosing in advance assume that what they'll want for lunch next week is a variety. And so they choose a turkey sandwich Monday, tuna on Tuesday, egg on Wednesday and so on. It turn out that when next week rolls around they generally don't like the variety they thought they would. In fact they are significantly less happy with their choices than the group who chose their sandwiches on the day.

People Cannot Predict Feelings

This variety versus sameness is only one particular bias that people display in making predictions about their future emotional states. There is another counter-intuitive bias emerging from the work being done in positive psychology. This looks at how people predict they will feel after both catastrophically bad, and, conversely, fantastically positive occurrences in their life. For example, how good would you feel if you won the lottery? Most people predict their lives will be completely changed and they'll be much happier. What does the research find? Yes, people are measurably happier after they've just won, but six months down the line they're back to their individual 'baseline' level of happiness.

So, in the journey from the sublime—predicting how we'll feel about winning the lottery—to the ridiculous—predicting which sandwiches we'll want for lunch—we are incredibly bad at knowing our future selves. And if we can't even decide what type of sandwich we might like next week, how can we possibly decide what type of job we'd like to be doing in twenty years?

With age occasionally comes wisdom. Over time we learn, whether implicitly or explicitly, that we are not that good at predicting the future. At the very least we begin to recognise it is a much less precise science than we once thought.

People Change over Time

This means your future self is probably a stranger to you. And, on some level, you know it. That's why it might be hard for an 18 year old to choose their career, but it's a damn sight harder for someone in midlife when limitations have been learnt.

This might seem like just another way of saying that people get more cautious as they get older, but it is more than that. It's actually saying that it's not caution that's increasing with age, but implicit self-knowledge. People begin to understand that the future holds vanishingly few certainties, even for those things that would seem to be under our most direct control, like our sandwich preferences.

The argument about miswanting applies to any area of our lives which involves making a prediction about what we might like in the future. Career planning becomes painful precisely because it's such an important decision and we come to understand that we have only very limited useful information.

The best strategy for career planning is this: make your best guess, try it out and don't be surprised if you don't like it. But for heaven's sake don't mention this in your interviews.

THREE

Raising the Compulsory High School Attendance Age Will Reduce Dropouts

Reg Weaver

Reg Weaver has served two terms as president of the 3.2-million-member National Education Association (NEA). He is a middle school science teacher with thirty years of classroom experience. In the following viewpoint Weaver states that the dropout age, which was set at the beginning of the 1900s, needs to be raised to serve the needs of society today. He indicates that the nation is paying the price for the low dropout age with a generation of young people who are more likely to be incarcerated than attend college. Sixteen-year-old students, who are too young to buy cigarettes or vote, should not be allowed to drop out of school.

One of the most distressing signs in American public education is the slow disappearance of students from high schools across this nation.

The statistics are staggering. Three out of every 10 public school students who started ninth grade in September will drop out of school before graduation.

Reg Weaver, "Curbing Dropouts by Raising the Exit Age," *San Diego Union Tribune*, October 6, 2006. Reproduced by permission of the author.

According to estimates, each day about seven thousand students nationwide drop out of high school.

This is a deadly number that is having devastating effects on America's young people, especially minority students. While the national graduation rate hovers around 70 percent, only about 50 percent of African-American, Hispanic and Native American students graduate with their class. Graduation rates also vary significantly among Asian and Pacific Islander ethnic groups.

Allowing Early Dropout Age Creates Crisis

With 30 percent of high school students slipping through the cracks of our educational system, educators and political leaders are looking for solutions. One answer worth exploring is making a high school diploma or its equivalent mandatory for all students below the age of 21.

Compulsory school attendance laws that allow students to quit school at 16 are unwitting enablers in the dropout crisis. This problem should be faced head-on by amending laws established when our nation's economy relied on farms and textile mills. How can public schools prepare students to compete in a global society when public education is guided by rules that date back to agrarian times?

According to estimates, about 1 million students fail to graduate from high school every year; that amounts to some 7,000 students who drop out of school each day.

Dropouts Cost the Nation

What happens when Johnny and his friends check out of school? Studies show that each class of high school dropouts costs the nation more than $200 billion in lost wages and tax revenues as well as spending for social support programs. They earn, on average, less than high school graduates and are more likely to be unemployed.

The earnings disadvantage that starts in their teen years often remains with them throughout their lives. Without the required education to obtain a good-paying job, high school dropouts face a bleak future: The majority of inmates in federal and state prisons failed to complete high school.

School Leaving Laws Have Several Components

An overview of compulsory attendance laws in the U.S. shows that many states have set the minimum age to leave school at 16, while others have upgraded their compulsory school laws to mandate school attendance until age 17 or 18.

Yet a closer look at the legislation reveals that there is much more to compulsory school laws than a specific age range within which students must remain in school. Even in states where the age has been raised, students can leave earlier than the legal minimum age if they work or receive parental consent.

While flexibility is needed to deal with special circumstances, research points to a need for more resolve in cases where students begin to disengage from high school. A Canadian study

Dropout Rates, 1972 to 2005

This chart shows the percentage of high school dropouts (status dropout, or those who are not enrolled and who have not earned a diploma or its equivalent) among persons 16 to 24 years old, by race/ethnicity.

| Year | Total | Race/Ethnicity | | |
		White	Black	Hispanic
1972	14.6	12.3	21.3	34.3
1980	14.1	11.4	19.1	35.2
1985	12.6	10.4	15.2	27.6
1990	12.1	9.0	13.2	32.4
1995	12.0	8.6	12.1	30.0
1996	11.1	7.3	13.0	29.4
1997	11.0	7.6	13.4	25.3
1998	11.8	7.7	13.8	29.5
1999	11.2	7.3	12.6	28.6
2000	10.9	6.9	13.1	27.8
2001	10.7	7.3	10.9	27.0
2002	10.5	6.5	11.3	25.7
2003	9.9	6.3	10.9	23.5
2004	10.3	6.8	11.8	23.8
2005	9.4	6.0	10.4	22.4

Includes other race/ethnicity categories not separately shown. . . . Beginning in 2003, respondents were able to identify as being more than one race. From 2003 onwards, the Black and White categories include individuals who considered themselves to be of only one race.

NOTE: The status dropout rate is the percentage of 16- through 24-year-olds who are not enrolled in high school and who lack a high school credential. A high school credential includes a high school diploma or equivalent credential, such as a General Educational Development (GED) certificate. Estimates beginning in 1987 reflect new editing procedures for cases with missing data on school enrollment items. Estimates beginning in 1992 reflect new wording of the educational attainment item. Estimates beginning in 1994 reflect changes due to newly instituted computer-assisted interviewing.

Taken from: U.S. Department of Education, National Center for Education Statistics, *The Condition of Education,* 2007.

that looked at the benefits of raising the minimum age for leaving school found that each additional year of compulsory schooling not only lowered the probability of being unemployed but also boosted weekly earnings.

Students Should Have to Earn a Diploma

Teachers, parents and public officials must reject the idea that it is acceptable for youngsters to drop out of school. Just as this country established compulsory attendance to the age of 16 or 17 in the beginning of the 20th century, it is appropriate and critical now to eradicate the idea of "dropping out" before achieving a diploma. This nation is paying the price—socially, economically and politically—for a generation that is more likely to be incarcerated than in college.

To reverse this trend, options such as high school graduation centers for students ages 19 to 21 should be readily available. In this setting, young adults can receive specialized instruction and counseling to effectively serve students in this age group. John Bridgeland of Civic Enterprises, who has studied attitudes among dropouts, says many of them would re-enroll if special programs for them existed.

Raising the school exit age alone is not the basis for a successful dropout prevention policy. To stem the growing dropout rate, schools must meet students' needs with a stimulating and relevant curriculum. And caring adults must step in and end the slow disengagement that leads 16-year-olds to opt out of their basic right to an education.

But raising the compulsory age for high school graduation or equivalency will help turn the tide on this silent epidemic. If 16 is too young to buy cigarettes and to vote, how can it be old enough to make such a life-changing decision?

FOUR

Raising the Compulsory High School Attendance Age Will Not Reduce Dropouts

Terry Stoops

Terry Stoops is an education policy analyst for the John Locke Foundation, which is a nonprofit, independent North Carolina organization that works for the future of the state. In the following viewpoint Stoops reviews extensive statistical reports from states with a range of compulsory attendance ages, stating his conclusions about the relationship of maximum attendance age to student graduation rates. He disagrees with proposals to raise the age at which students can legally drop out of high school. He asserts that enforcing existing truancy laws for public school students who have not reached the age of sixteen is preferable to paying the cost of trying to keep unwilling students in school for a longer period.

The compulsory attendance age is the age in which students are legally required to attend school. Once they meet the maximum attendance age, students are typically free to drop out of school, en-

Terry Stoops, "Raise the Bar, Not the Age," *Spotlight*, May 31, 2007. Reproduced by permission of the John Locke Foundation.

ter the workplace, find an alternative route to earn a high school diploma, or earn a General Educational Development (GED) credential. Currently, North Carolina is among the 26 states that have a maximum compulsory age of 16. Nine states set the age at 17, and 15 states and D.C. have a compulsory age of 18.

Education attendance laws vary by state, but nearly all states have some kind of exemption from compulsory attendance laws. Students who graduate, have employment, participate in an exit interview, or obtain parents' permission may be eligible for exemption from the attendance laws. Thus, the maximum compulsory attendance age often serves as a guideline rather than an absolute.

There Is Misinformation About the Effects of Raising Attendance Age

Among legislators in North Carolina, there is a great deal of misinformation about the effect of raising the compulsory attendance age on student retention. Rep. Angela Bryant, a Democrat who represents the counties of Halifax and Nash, is one [of] the primary sponsors of House Bill 1790, "Raise Compulsory Education Age & Graduation Rate." If enacted, the bill would appoint a 27-member task force to study the educational, programmatic, legal, and fiscal issues toward raising the compulsory age to 17 by 2009 and age 18 by 2011. In addition, the task force would be called to "identify best practices to provide racial equity in opportunities to stay in and succeed in school and to eliminate the barriers of racism, classism, sexism and other 'ISMS' that can impact the 16–18 year olds" targeted by the bill.

Rep. Bryant believes that the true value of the bill lies in the fact that it makes "a cultural and institutional statement" about the value of school. Like other bills proposing to raise the attendance age, House Bill 1790 is steeped in promises but short on details. For example, Rep. Bryant is unsure whether raising the maximum compulsory attendance age would increase the graduation rate, leaving those questions to the task force to study. Nevertheless, she maintains great hope that the bill would increase attendance, thereby increasing the graduation rate. During a recent committee

Many high schools in states like North Carolina have insti-tuted compulsory attendance mandates to keep students in school.

meeting, she reasoned, "we really don't know if it will increase the graduation rate, but we can't increase the graduation rate if the kids aren't there." While she does not know about the effect of the bill on the graduation rate, Rep. Bryant claims that the bill could reduce instances of HIV and arthritis.

Attendance Age May Not Affect Graduation Rate

While it would be difficult to assess the effect of compulsory attendance laws on instances of HIV and arthritis, there are a great deal of data that could be used to determine if compulsory attendance age requirements have an effect on graduation and dropout rates. First, there is no apparent relationship between the maximum compulsory age and graduation rates.

While four of the top five states with the highest graduation rate have a compulsory attendance age of 16, a number of states with a compulsory attendance age of 16 have a relatively low graduation rate. Similarly, states with a compulsory attendance age of 17 or 18 have graduation rates that rank toward the top and the bottom of the list. In this way, an attendance age of 18 provides no guarantee of a better graduation rate than a compulsory attendance age [of] 16 or 17.

The same is true with dropout rates. States with a compulsory attendance age of 16 do not necessarily have high dropout rates. One of the two lowest dropout rates belongs to a state (New Jersey) that has a compulsory attendance age of 16. On the other hand, the state with the highest dropout rate in the nation (Louisiana) has a compulsory attendance age of 18.

Given the fact that no observable relationship can be established between attendance age and dropout rate, North Carolina's low graduation rate and high dropout rate have little to do with the compulsory attendance age. Legislation aimed at increasing the compulsory attendance age to 17 or 18 will do little to solve North Carolina's graduation and dropout crisis.

Taken as a whole, states with a compulsory attendance age of 16 have higher average and median graduation rates than states with an attendance age of 17 and 18. Similarly, states with a compulsory attendance age of 16 have average and median dropout rates comparable to states with an attendance age of 17 and 18.

Research agrees that increasing the compulsory attendance age does not guarantee an increase in the graduation rate or a

Percentage of Average and Median Graduation and Dropout Rates in the United States

Maximum Compulsory Attendance Age	Average Graduation Rate	Median Graduation Rate	Average Dropout Rate	Median Dropout Rate
16 years old	71.7	72.9	4.0	3.55
17 years old	67.2	71.8	4.1	3.4
18 years old	70.4	71.0	4.0	3.5
U.S. and D.C. average	69.6	72.3	4.0	3.4

Taken from: Terry Stoops, "Raise the Bar, Not the Age," *Spotlight*, May 31, 2007.

decline in the dropout rate. Professor Rosemary J. Avery of Cornell University analyzed dropout and graduation rates before and after four states raised their compulsory attendance age. In her analysis, none of the states increased their graduation rate. Dropout data for Minnesota and Wyoming also showed no improvement attributed to the change.

Raising Compulsory Attendance Age Costs Money

Avery also noted the additional costs required to raise the compulsory attendance age, including hiring and training new teachers, building more classrooms and larger facilities, and providing transportation for the initial increase in student enrollment. The likelihood that some students would drop out of school regardless of the change means that investments in teachers, facilities, and transportation would go to waste. Thus, she concluded,

> Raising the compulsory school attendance age would not be a cost effective mandate in terms of achieving its intended goals. Statistical data support that a change would not significantly increase the high-school completion rates and reduce dropout rates. Also, there are sizable costs associated with implementing such a program including spending on new teachers, facilities, and transportation for projected, but not necessarily enduring, increases in student enrollment.

Given the lack of evidence that this policy change is effective, North Carolina should seek other policy avenues for increasing the graduation rate or lowering the dropout rate. . . .

State Legislatures Analyze Costs

Proposals to increase the maximum attendance age in North Carolina have neglected to outline the fiscal impact of such a policy. Other state legislatures have analyzed the costs associated with raising the compulsory attendance age and have found that the costs of retaining additional students were substantial.

- A 1998 fiscal note from the state of Kentucky found that the cost of retaining 50 percent of the students who would not return to school on their own initiative (5,200 students) would be $15,204,800. The cost doubles if none of the students (10,400 students) would return to school on their own initiative. Given the substantial costs associated with the change, the Kentucky legislature did not pass the bill that would have increased the compulsory attendance age.

- A detailed 2006 fiscal impact report from the state of Colorado indicated that state and local government would incur $1.9 million per year in additional costs related to retaining 265 students affected by the change in the compulsory attendance law. The expenses included additional costs for monitoring truancy cases ($369.81 per student) and added state and local per-pupil funding ($6,800 per student).

- A 2006 fiscal note from the state of Florida estimated that the cost of increasing the compulsory attendance age from 16 to 18 would initially cost taxpayers $311.1 million and require recurring annual operating cost of approximately $89 million. While this figure was a best-case scenario (i.e., a complete cessation in school dropouts between the ages of 16 and 18), retaining just 25 percent of the dropouts would cost the state an estimated $77.8 million initially and $22.3 million annually.

- A 2007 fiscal note from the state of Iowa showed that the state would be required to allocate approximately $1.4 million for the first year and $1.5 million for the second year of increasing the maximum compulsory attendance age from 16 to 18. The fiscal note estimated that the state would have to provide services for 258 additional students at a cost of $5,546 per student for the first year and $5,768 per student for the second year. It did not estimate the increased legal and court costs associated with the change, but said that "Raising the age for compulsory school attendance may create issues for truancy with the potential for mediation, civil penalties and court involvement."

Estimated 942 Students Will Cost $8.46 Million

In North Carolina, it would cost at least an additional $8.46 million a year to cover the additional cost of services for an estimated 942 students that would be affected by an increase in the compulsory attendance age to 17 years old. A bill to increase the attendance age to 18 would incur even greater costs.

As noted above, it is difficult to estimate the court costs required to review and adjudicate additional truancy cases. Researchers at the Colorado legislature estimated that an increase in the compulsory attendance age would require an additional $370 per student in legal costs. Applying that figure to North Carolina, the legislature would have to appropriate nearly $350,000 a year to the state's courts to cover for the increased burden that the increase would place upon our justice system. Thus, raising the compulsory attendance age to 17 would cost North Carolina taxpayers approximately $8.8 million.

Little Will Be Gained Forcing Students to Stay in School

An April 2007 poll by the J.W.P. Civitas Institute found that 72 percent of respondents supported an increase in the mandatory attendance age from 16 to 18. This finding suggests that the public is misinformed about the effect of the compulsory attendance age on student retention. Wayward legislators, school system officials, and public school advocacy groups, in particular, say that an increase in the attendance age would compel students to stay in school. Yet this notion is not informed by research that shows otherwise. There is very little to be gained by forcing unruly or indifferent students to stay longer in schools that are not meeting their needs.

Efforts to reach out to students at risk of dropping out must begin in the elementary and middle school grades. In particular, school systems and law enforcement officials must begin earnestly enforcing existing truancy laws for public school students who have not reached 16 years of age but are chronically absent from school. When parents and young public school students are not held accountable for violating truancy laws, the state engages in a de facto endorsement of chronic absenteeism.

FIVE

College Is Not for Everyone

Thomas Reeves

> In the following viewpoint Thomas Reeves suggests that
> the drive to send all high school students to college is mis-
> guided. Many high school graduates, Reeves maintains, are
> ill-prepared for college. Reeves asserts that a large percent-
> age of such students eventually drop out, and their presence
> in college classrooms lowers academic standards. Many
> high school students are better suited to learning a trade
> and should not be pushed into a college education. Reeves
> is a fellow at the Wisconsin Policy Research Institute
> and the author of several books, including *A Question of
> Character: A Life of John F. Kennedy* and *America's Bishop:
> The Biography of Archbishop Fulton J. Sheen*.

A billboard I saw recently featured the photograph of a smil-
ing woman and under it, in large letters, the boast that she
has sent nineteen young people to college. Whether this was
an advertisement for a bank or a charitable organization, the
thought occurred to me, a veteran of forty years of college teaching, that the act itself, while on the surface laudable, might not
have been a wise investment of time and money.

Thomas Reeves, "Some Heretical Thoughts for a New Academic Year," National Association of
Scholars Online Forum, August 25, 2003. Reproduced by permission.

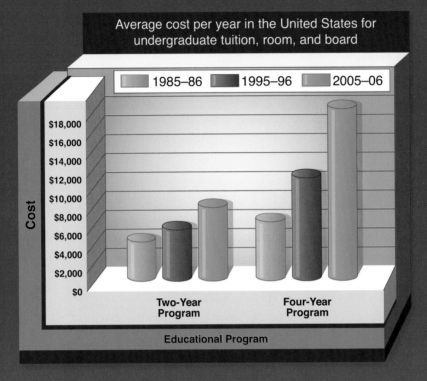

Annual Cost of College

Average cost per year in the United States for undergraduate tuition, room, and board

Legend: 1985–86 | 1995–96 | 2005–06

Y-axis (Cost): $0, $2,000, $4,000, $6,000, $8,000, $10,000, $12,000, $14,000, $16,000, $18,000

X-axis (Educational Program): Two-Year Program, Four-Year Program

Taken from: U.S. Department of Education, National Center for Education Statistics, 2007.

College Is a Fad

Going to college has become a national fad, a rite of passage, millions hope, into the world of hefty salaries and McMansions. The trek to academia has now spread to the working class, who see sending their kids to college as a sign of respectability, like vacationing in Branson, Missouri, owning an SUV, and having a weed-free lawn with a gazing globe. Minorities too are getting into the act, being wooed and financially rewarded by campus administrators to meet institutional racial quotas. But is this crush for diplomas necessarily a good thing? Is it always a prudent investment, for the individual and for society, to be sending junior off to the dorm?

Not All Students Are Prepared for College

Let us consider our nineteen new college students. In the first place, how many of them have the intellect and the intellectual preparation to be serious and successful students? ACT scores continue to decline nationally, and Richard T. Ferguson, ACT's chief executive, urges better high school preparation. About four in ten last year [2002] scored well enough on the test to suggest that they could earn at least a C in a college-level math course. On tenth grade math tests in Wisconsin recently, 76 percent of white students attained proficiency or better, compared with 40 percent of Hispanics, and 23 percent of blacks. In Michigan, Colorado, Texas, and New York, academic tests have been altered or thrown out because of low scores. The great majority of high schools continue to require little in exchange for their diplomas. Hundreds of thousands enter the campus gates without a clue about the intellectual challenges that are, or at least should be, awaiting them.

The impact on college and university campuses of legions of unprepared freshmen is never positive. Millions of dollars must be spent annually in remedial education. And the rate of failure is still extraordinarily high. The ACT estimates that one in four fail or drop out after one year. A third of the freshmen at the relatively select University of Wisconsin-Madison do not return for a second year. I toiled for decades on a Wisconsin campus on which a mere 18 percent of the entering freshmen ever graduate. The financial costs, let alone the emotional toll on the young people involved, [are] scandalous.

Admitting Unprepared Students Lowers Academic Standards

Even more important is the impact of intellectually unprepared people on the educational process itself. Anti-intellectualism is the Great Enemy of the educator, and with a classroom full of people who do not read, study, or think, academic standards inevitably suffer. In an article titled "The Classroom Game," I described my own tribulations with students in an open-admissions environment. The most well-intentioned professor cannot educate those who refuse to be educated. All too often, such students demand that they be passed through the system and awarded a diploma, as they were in high school.

The well-documented proliferation of stuff and nonsense for academic credit in large part stems from the admission of masses of ill-prepared students. Why take a lab science, a foreign language, or (for real diversity) the history of foreign countries if these courses aren't required? Why take classes with written examinations and term papers when most do not? That almost no one cares about the denigration of academic standards in higher education is also scandalous.

Every year colleges admit students who are educationally unprepared to enter college.

And what colleges and universities did our nineteen students on the billboard attend? Did they go where leftist indoctrination is their daily food and drink? Probably. It is difficult to find alternatives these days. When the University of California Academic Assembly recently dropped its requirement for professors to be impartial and dispassionate, it was simply acknowledging the abandonment of efforts to be objective. A San Diego schoolteacher, whose son complained about leftist bias in a class he took at the local UC campus, commented, "I'm very concerned about the changes. This gives much greater latitude to those professors who would use the classroom as a personal bully pulpit. UC students and the people of California deserve better." So do young people and taxpayers all over the country.

There Are Alternatives to College

In America and all across the Western world, intellectuals are enthralled with the abolition of moral and intellectual standards. In the courts and in the media, as well as the classroom, they are ramming this dogma down the throats of the vast majority. Are our nineteen students better off for being enveloped by the very poison that is slowly killing our civilization? Are we by definition doing them a favor by sending them to college? They may earn more during their lifetimes. But at what cost?

Shortages in skilled labor abound. Why not a billboard boasting that, say, eight of our nineteen young people have been sent to tech schools, have learned trades, and are currently in the work force leading productive lives and earning good wages? Is a machinist or a carpenter any less of a respectable American than someone who spent six years studying Mass Communications and Anthropology? In my judgment, we say so at our national peril.

I recently read about an auto mechanic whose high school counselor told him that he was ruining his life by opting for vocational training. The young man is now in great demand in the job market, works extremely hard, and makes over $100,000 a year. He is a happy and productive citizen. Did he waste his life? Not in this old professor's book.

SIX

Students with Disabilities Can Find Good Jobs with the Proper Support

Sean Roy and Beth Casper

> Sean Roy and Beth Casper work at the PACER Center, a Minneapolis-based parent training and information center for families of children and youth with disabilities, from birth through age twenty-one. In the following viewpoint Roy and Casper examine ways for young people with disabilities to develop career skills and gain their first employment. The authors emphasize the importance of taking advantage of community networks and gaining on-the-job experience through volunteering.

Young people looking for their first jobs may be overwhelmed by the process and seek help from others. Individualized Education Program (IEP) teams can help young people with disabilities develop a plan that includes employment goals. Schools can also help youth develop specific career skills by guiding students to courses needed to enter a particular field, helping students practice interviewing and asking for employment accommodations, or offering work-based learning opportunities.

Sean Roy and Beth Casper, "Promoting Effective Parent Involvement in Secondary Education and Transition," *Parent Brief*, March 2006. Reproduced by permission of National Center on Secondary Education, Institute on Community Integration, University of Minnesota.

Work-based learning during the school years leads to better postschool employment outcomes. Volunteer experiences and unpaid internships, in addition to paid employment, can be steppingstones to future employment. Youth and their families need not rely solely on school programs to pursue such opportunities. They can do much on their own to launch the youth's career search. Recent studies demonstrate the effectiveness of using personal networks as a job search strategy, and highlight the fact that families make key contributions to successful employment outcomes for individuals with disabilities (26th Institute on Rehabilitation Issues, 2000).

Networks Help Young People with Disabilities Find Employment

There are creative ways to combine community relationships, a young person's interests, and family or personal networks to help a young person effectively explore work-based learning outside of school settings. Parents may seek opportunities through co-workers, relatives, and neighbors. Moreover, parents often know their children better than professionals do and can help their sons and daughters explore their unique abilities, strengths, and interests—all of which may lead to an appropriate career path.

Many practical strategies for preparing a young adult with disabilities for employment are not difficult. These include such things as assigning chores at home, encouraging youth to volunteer in their community, or keeping an eye open for employment opportunities. Families can adopt these or other approaches within their own communities or share their ideas with the IEP team. The insights of family members can serve as the basis for strategies and services identified in a student's IEP transition goals. Youth can also learn to be self-advocates in seeking a good job.

Youth with Disabilities Can Take Control

Ultimately, to be successful in the workplace, youth must develop skills that allow them to become as independent as possible. Skills such as self-knowledge, goal setting, decision making, problem solving, and self-advocacy are crucial for young people with disabilities. These skills are all considered aspects of self-determination. Research supports the idea that youth who leave high school with self-determination skills have a greater chance of achieving positive postschool outcomes than those who do not. Self-determined youth will also be able to exert greater control in the selection and use of adult services and supports in their postsecondary education and employment goals.

Parents can help their children develop self-determination skills by creating a supportive environment, which allows youth to take risks, test their abilities and limitations, develop their problem solving skills, and practice positive work habits and behaviors. Although parents can do much to launch their sons and daughters into the work force, their children's future is their own. An understanding of oneself, including how one's health and disability will impact work, is key to becoming an effective self-advocate and essential to postsecondary education and employment success.

Juan: Taking the Initiative

Juan, an 18-year-old who grew up in Mexico, recently moved to Minneapolis with his family. Although Juan dropped out of school before earning his diploma, he received four years of education in the United States and had been diagnosed with a learning disability. He wanted to increase his employability by gaining work skills and experience, but he also worried that the lack of a diploma would be an obstacle to a job that pays well. One day a friend told him about a work program at a local community center, and Juan decided to check it out. The program was a youth employment and training program funded by the Workforce Investment Act (WIA). The staff helped Juan to earn his GED [General Educational Development, the equivalent of a high school diploma], increase his work-readiness skills, and understand his disability and how it might affect his work style. Now Juan feels prepared to explain his learning disability and ask for appropriate accommodations once he is offered a job.

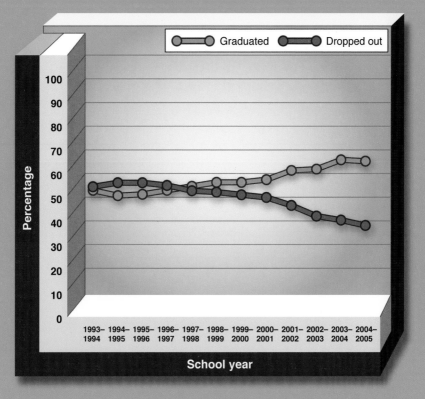

Graduation and Dropout Rates for Students with Disabilities

Graduated — **Dropped out**

Percentage

School year
1993–1994
1994–1995
1995–1996
1996–1997
1997–1998
1998–1999
1999–2000
2000–2001
2001–2002
2002–2003
2003–2004
2004–2005

17.8 percent decrease in dropout rates
11 percent increase in graduation rates

Taken from: Individuals with Disabilities Education Act (IDEA) Data, 2006.

Youth Must Explore Their Skills and Interests

Starting a journey toward successful employment may seem more difficult than the journey itself. Often young people blossom once they are given a chance to prove themselves, and a career path is more easily identified using the new knowledge of their skills and interests.

Parents can help organize and clarify a young person's strengths, needs, and interests. Keep in mind a student's skills and preferences:

• Perceptual skills: ability to judge where, how, and if things fit together.

- Interpersonal skills: attitude, cooperation, teamwork, and communication skills. Look at how a student gets along with family, people in the community, peers, teachers, and employers.
- Work aptitudes: ability to remember and follow instructions and procedures; ability to plan, organize, and improve with practice.

Parents of disabled children can help them develop self-determination skills by creating a supportive environment.

- Work behaviors: ability to concentrate and stay on a task and ability to remain motivated.
- Interests: personal goals and interests, hobbies, leisure-time activities, academics, and favorite and least-favorite subjects.
- Cognitive skills: reading and math skills, concept formation, thinking style, and problem solving abilities.
- Motor skills: using one's hands, eye/hand coordination, fine motor skills, and mobility.

It is also important to talk with a young person about his or her dreams. A young person should answer questions such as: What do I do well? What is hard for me? What do I like to do?

Maria: What Kind of Job Do I Want?

Maria, 18, wanted to get a summer job, but she didn't know what she wanted to do. Her father realized the importance of finding employment for Maria that suited her strengths and interests. He knew that, because of her developmental disability, Maria might not be successful in a job where she felt pressured or one where she had to follow multiple directives. Before Maria started looking for summer employment, she and her father explored her expectations for a career. They were able to identify that Maria preferred to work outside, in a casual environment, and have a flexible schedule. Maria also expressed concerns that she would not be able to count change; she did not want to work as a cashier. With this information, Maria and her father started the job search and found a part-time position at a tree farm. The time Maria and her father spent talking about careers, her interests, and her likes and dislikes helped her focus the job search and find a summer job she really liked. It also gave her a head start on developing an Individual Plan for Employment with the counselor from the state vocational rehabilitation agency that she will begin working with in the fall.

Volunteering Experience Makes an Applicant Appealing

Paid work experience is not the only thing that makes a job applicant's résumé appealing to an employer. Employers appreciate a young person who shows the motivation to do a good job. Youth who may be too young or not ready for a paid job can create a résumé and gain valuable experience by doing jobs around the house or neighborhood or by volunteering even for a day. Including a list of informational interviews conducted by youth in a résumé can also help document an individual's initiative as well as vocational education experiences. Parents can help youth identify the types of experiences that may be included in the youth's résumé.

Adam: Résumé and References

Adam, who is 14 and has Down Syndrome, was too young to have a job, but he was eagerly looking forward to finding a job the following year. He had learned about résumés in school but wondered what he could list on one since he had no previous employment. However, Adam had been mowing several lawns in the neighborhood, and his mother suggested that he ask some of his clients for a reference letter. After making sure that he was on time and did a good job with every lawn all summer, Adam asked his neighbors if they might provide him with letters. To his amazement everyone was willing. He was proud of the letters that highlighted his hard work and his traits of being prompt and considerate. The next summer he took the letters with him to an interview at a lawn-care service. The manager was extremely impressed and offered Adam a job.

Shayla: Looking Ahead

Shayla, 20, has a chronic health condition. She currently works 12 hours a week busing tables at a restaurant. She appreciates having the job and the spending money it provides, but she is also interested in exploring other vocations. At school, she participated in a career interest assessment, which her parents helped her complete. The assessment noted that she would enjoy the responsibility and organization of office work. Shayla agreed and asked her parents if they knew anyone who worked in an office. She had learned about informational interviews in school and wanted to conduct one with someone who worked in her field of interest. Her uncle, a warehouse shipping supervisor, arranged for Shayla to speak to the office manager. Not only did she learn about office work, she also gained an experience to add to her résumé. Shayla is currently taking office skills classes in school and plans to look for an office job when she graduates.

Job Satisfaction

Matching a person's strengths and interests to a job is important to ensuring long-term success and job satisfaction. Youth should explore vocations that interest them. Matching youth with jobs that suit their interests and strengths is one way to promote success in the workplace.

There Are Numerous Supports for Youth with Disabilities

Many youth with significant disabilities use job coaches, assistive technology, and/or workplace accommodations when entering employment. These formal supports can be provided or funded by service providers from special education, county social services, waiver programs, vocational rehabilitation, or developmental disabilities systems. Formal supports can be short term or extend long into the course of an individual's employment. Parents and youth should also be aware of natural supports that may be available in the workplace. Natural supports include training, job sharing, mentoring, and flexible scheduling. An example of a natural support is when a more experienced employee helps a co-worker solve a problem. Natural supports are provided directly by the employer (not an outside agency) and may be generally available to employees who are not disabled. Natural supports are appealing to employers because they are generally low cost. They are also appealing to people with disabilities and their families because they promote normal interaction and relationships with co-workers.

Involving co-workers in support of employment is important even when an individual requires formal supports from an outside agency. Employees with disabilities who receive natural supports from co-workers are more likely to have more typical work roles, higher wages, and positive relationships with co-workers. It may require some effort to find the right situation for a person who needs extra support on the job, but once in place, a system of natural supports can increase the feelings of accomplishment and independence on the job for a person with a disability.

Barbara: Personal Connections Build Natural Supports

Barbara, 16, has a moderate cognitive disability. She was very excited about having a job but required a certain level of on-the-job training and supervision to be successful. A job coach was not available through her special education program, and Barbara did not yet qualify for other services to pay for a job coach. One day while grocery shopping, Barbara's mother noticed her arranging disheveled stock on the shelves and tending to empty shopping carts. The next day Barbara's mother called the store and spoke to the manager. The manager knew that Barbara's family were long-time customers and was willing to give Barbara a job on a trial basis. The manager was also willing to recruit other workers in the store to act as Barbara's support staff. Now, Barbara not only has a job, but she has also gained many friends who help her every day. She doesn't need much help now that she has mastered most of the daily tasks of her work at the store. . . .

Using Your Personal Network

Most people have a circle of contacts within a community. Relatives, friends, co-workers, and people who own or work at the grocery stores, restaurants, or other businesses regularly patronized by a family can have potential job leads. Think outside of your close friends and acquaintances. The personal contacts of IEP team members may also lead to independent job opportunities. The vast majority of jobs are gained not by responding to an advertisement in the newspaper, but by using contacts. Using this method can also help identify safe and familiar work site locations. Don't despair if this method does not yield results right away. Sometimes notifying friends and acquaintances will prompt them to think of you when a job opportunity arises in the future.

John: Spreading the Word

John, a 16-year-old with spina bifida, was hoping to find a summer job. Spanish was both a strong interest and an academic strength of John's, and he had previously identified improving his Spanish language ability as an IEP goal. He hoped to find a summer job that would help him build his Spanish-speaking skills. Because he uses a wheelchair, John would also need to find a setting that was wheelchair accessible. He mentioned his goal at his IEP meeting his junior year. A district administrator attending John's IEP meeting was a close friend of a principal at a Spanish immersion elementary school that conducted an annual summer camp—in a school building that had recently been renovated to meet the accessibility standards of the Americans with Disabilities Act. Hearing of John's interest, the administrator called her friend, who welcomed the idea of having a student volunteer. Personal connections helped create a successful volunteer opportunity for John at the summer camp—and eventually a part-time job the following year.

Josh: Getting By with a Little Help from Friends

Josh is a 16-year-old with a significant learning disability. He is also an avid sports fan. Josh received special education services in school. He identified the goal of exploring employment opportunities in a sports-related field with his IEP team during the school year. When Josh expressed an interest in finding a summer job, he and his parents began his job search by brainstorming ideas for jobs he might like—such as working at a health club, selling sports equipment, or working at the baseball stadium, or a park and recreation summer program. Next, he and his parents mapped a network of contacts, identifying relatives, friends, and co-workers, who might have leads. In all they listed 20 people they could ask about opportunities for Josh. The husband of a co-worker knew of a part-time opening as a golf course attendant. Josh was able to land the job. Josh was thrilled, because he loves watching Tiger Woods on television.

Building Confidence Through Volunteering

Learning on the job is the best way to develop job skills. However, young people with disabilities may need help obtaining real work experience. School guidance counselors, religious leaders, or friends may know of job shadowing, volunteer, or internship opportunities for youth. When young people feel too insecure to find volunteer work on their own, parents or other family members can help them overcome their initial anxiety by offering to volunteer together. Through experience, youth will see they have the ability to work on their own.

Calvin: Volunteering Opens Doors

Calvin, 16, was looking for his first job but was having difficulty finding one. Jobs in his neighborhood were scarce. Although he had a hearing impairment, he did not receive services that would help him find a part-time job after school hours. One evening, Calvin's mother mentioned his situation to a cousin, who works as the kitchen supervisor for a local retirement residence. Calvin's cousin suggested that Calvin gain some work experience by volunteering there on the weekends. At first Calvin only prepared for and cleaned up after lunches on Saturdays, but soon he was asked if he could work more hours. Calvin was such a hard worker that he was offered a paying position in the kitchen. Now, because of his upbeat attitude and strong work ethic, he is a favorite among staff and residents.

Robert: Volunteer Experiences Build a Résumé

Robert is an active 15-year-old with Attention Deficit Disorder. Over the summer, students in Robert's high school work-skills class were encouraged to add one volunteer work experience to their résumé. One day, Robert's brother saw an ad recruiting volunteers to work at an upcoming marathon. Robert loves spending time in the out of doors, but was nervous about responding on his own. He agreed, however, when his brother said he would volunteer along with him. Both brothers were assigned responsibility for filling and distributing water at a point on the race route. Robert had so much fun that he worked by himself at three other races and one family-fun day at the health club that summer. Robert impressed his work-skills teacher by having five volunteer experiences on his résumé. He continues to volunteer and has applied for a paying position at the health club.

Building the Foundation for Self Determination

Youth with disabilities who participate in quality work-based learning activities have more successful post-school outcomes, including employment and further education. Real-life work experiences help a young person develop important "soft skills" such as teamwork and time management, make career decisions, network with potential employers, and develop job skills relevant to future employment. They also help youth assess the impact of their disability in an employment setting and learn what job accommodations they need in the workplace. Using their combined resources, youth, families, and IEP teams can ensure that work-based learning opportunities are a good match with a student's individual interests, strengths, and needs. These experiences not only help youth to build their résumés, but provide the foundation for a life of increased earning and self determination.

SEVEN

The Rights of Students with Disabilities at Postsecondary Institutions

U.S. Department of Education, Office for Civil Rights

> The following viewpoint, prepared by the U.S. Department of Education's Office for Civil Rights, provides a guide to the laws covering students with disabilities in postsecondary programs, including vocational and career schools, two- and four-year colleges, and universities. The authors assert that students with disabilities pursuing postsecondary education should be knowledgeable about their responsibilities and about the school's responsibilities to them. For example, the authors explain that postsecondary institutions cannot discriminate against students based on their disability, and schools must make certain academic adjustments at the request of students with disabilities.

More and more high school students with disabilities are planning to continue their education in postsecondary schools, including vocational and career schools, two- and four-year colleges, and universities. As a student with a disability, you need to be well informed about your rights and responsibilities as well as the responsibilities postsecondary schools have toward

U.S. Department of Education, "Students with Disabilities Preparing for Postsecondary Education: Know Your Rights and Responsibilities," March 2007.

you. Being well informed will help ensure you have a full opportunity to enjoy the benefits of the postsecondary education experience without confusion or delay.

[This] information . . . , provided by the Office for Civil Rights (OCR) in the U. S. Department of Education, explains the rights and responsibilities of students with disabilities who are preparing to attend postsecondary schools. This [viewpoint] also explains the obligations of a postsecondary school to provide academic adjustments, including auxiliary aids and services, to ensure the school does not discriminate on the basis of disability.

The Rehabilitation Act of 1973 Prohibits Discrimination

OCR enforces Section 504 of the Rehabilitation Act of 1973 (Section 504) and Title II of the Americans with Disabilities Act of 1990 (Title II), which prohibit discrimination on the basis of disability. Practically every school district and postsecondary

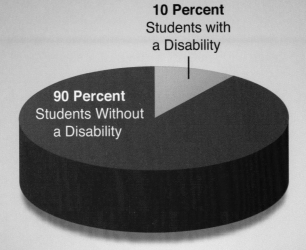

Disabled and Nondisabled Postsecondary Students, 2004

10 Percent
Students with a Disability

90 Percent
Students Without a Disability

Taken from: American Association of People with Disabilities (AAPD), "Groundbreaking Report Reveals Major Obstacles to College Access Nationwide for Students with Disabilities," July 2004. www.aapd-dc.org.

school in the United States is subject to one or both of these laws, which have similar requirements.

Although both school districts and postsecondary schools must comply with these same laws, the responsibilities of postsecondary schools are significantly different from those of school districts.

Moreover, you will have responsibilities as a postsecondary student that you do not have as a high school student. OCR strongly encourages you to know your responsibilities and those of postsecondary schools under Section 504 and Title II. Doing so will improve your opportunity to succeed as you enter postsecondary education.

The following questions and answers provide more specific information to help you succeed.

As a student with a disability leaving high school and entering postsecondary education, will I see differences in my rights and how they are addressed? Yes. Section 504 and Title II protect elementary, secondary and postsecondary students from discrimination. Nevertheless, several of the requirements that apply through high school are different from the requirements that apply beyond high school. For instance, Section 504 requires a school district to provide a free appropriate public education (FAPE) to each child with a disability in the district's jurisdiction. Whatever the disability, a school district must identify an individual's education needs and provide any regular or special education and related aids and services necessary to meet those needs as well as it is meeting the needs of students without disabilities.

Unlike your high school, your postsecondary school is not required to provide FAPE. Rather, your postsecondary school is required to provide appropriate academic adjustments as necessary to ensure that it does not discriminate on the basis of disability. In addition, if your postsecondary school provides housing to nondisabled students, it must provide comparable, convenient and accessible housing to students with disabilities at the same cost.

Other important differences you need to know, even before you arrive at your postsecondary school, are addressed in the remaining questions.

May a postsecondary school deny my admission because I have a disability? No. If you meet the essential requirements for admission, a postsecondary school may not deny your admission simply because you have a disability.

Do I have to inform a postsecondary school that I have a disability? No. However, if you want the school to provide an academic adjustment, you must identify yourself as having a disability. Likewise, you should let the school know about your disability if you want to ensure that you are assigned to accessible facilities. In any event, your disclosure of a disability is always voluntary.

What academic adjustments must a postsecondary school provide? The appropriate academic adjustment must be determined based on your disability and individual needs. Academic adjustments may include auxiliary aids and modifications to academic requirements as are necessary to ensure equal educational opportunity. Examples of such adjustments are arranging for priority registration;

A visually-impaired college student uses a portable video magnifier to read as part of a program sponsored by Virginia Tech to show disabled students how to overcome their disabilities.

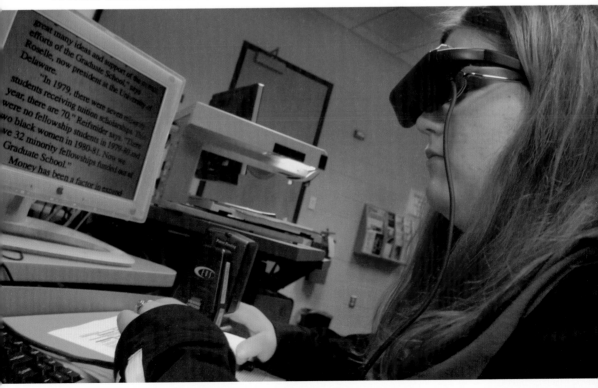

reducing a course load; substituting one course for another; providing note takers, recording devices, sign language interpreters, extended time for testing and, if telephones are provided in dorm rooms, a TTY [teletypewriter, a device enabling those with hearing impairments to use a telephone] in your dorm room; and equipping school computers with screen-reading, voice recognition or other adaptive software or hardware.

In providing an academic adjustment, your postsecondary school is not required to lower or effect substantial modifications to essential requirements. For example, although your school may be required to provide extended testing time, it is not required to change the substantive content of the test. In addition, your postsecondary school does not have to make modifications that would fundamentally alter the nature of a service, program or activity or would result in undue financial or administrative burdens. Finally, your postsecondary school does not have to provide personal attendants, individually prescribed devices, readers for personal use or study, or other devices or services of a personal nature, such as tutoring and typing.

If I want an academic adjustment, what must I do? You must inform the school that you have a disability and need an academic adjustment. Unlike your school district, your postsecondary school is not required to identify you as having a disability or assess your needs.

Your postsecondary school may require you to follow reasonable procedures to request an academic adjustment. You are responsible for knowing and following these procedures. Postsecondary schools usually include, in their publications providing general information, information on the procedures and contacts for requesting an academic adjustment. Such publications include recruitment materials, catalogs and student handbooks, and are often available on school Web sites. Many schools also have staff whose purpose is to assist students with disabilities. If you are unable to locate the procedures, ask a school official, such as an admissions officer or counselor.

When should I request an academic adjustment? Although you may request an academic adjustment from your postsecondary school at any time, you should request it as early as possible. Some academic adjustments may take more time to provide than others. You should follow your school's procedures to ensure that your school has enough time to review your request and provide an appropriate academic adjustment.

Do I have to prove that I have a disability to obtain an academic adjustment? Generally, yes. Your school will probably require you to provide documentation that shows you have a current disability and need an academic adjustment.

What documentation should I provide? Schools may set reasonable standards for documentation. Some schools require more documentation than others. They may require you to provide documentation prepared by an appropriate professional, such as a medical doctor, psychologist or other qualified diagnostician. The required documentation may include one or more of the following: a diagnosis of your current disability; the date of the diagnosis; how the diagnosis was reached; the credentials of the professional; how your disability affects a major life activity; and how the disability affects your academic performance. The documentation should provide enough information for you and your school to decide what is an appropriate academic adjustment.

Although an individualized education program (IEP) or Section 504 plan, if you have one, may help identify services that have been effective for you, it generally is not sufficient documentation. This is because postsecondary education presents different demands than high school education, and what you need to meet these new demands may be different. Also in some cases, the nature of a disability may change.

If the documentation that you have does not meet the postsecondary school's requirements, a school official should tell you in a timely manner what additional documentation you need to provide. You may need a new evaluation in order to provide the required documentation.

Who has to pay for a new evaluation? Neither your high school nor your postsecondary school is required to conduct or pay for a new evaluation to document your disability and need for an academic adjustment. This may mean that you have to pay or find funding to pay an appropriate professional for an evaluation. If you are eligible for services through your state vocational rehabilitation agency, you may qualify for an evaluation at no cost to you . . . .

Once the school has received the necessary documentation from me, what should I expect? The school will review your request in light of the essential requirements for the relevant program to help determine an appropriate academic adjustment. It is important to remember that the school is not required to lower or waive essential requirements. If you have requested a specific academic adjustment, the school may offer that academic adjustment or an alternative one if the alternative would also be effective. The school may also conduct its own evaluation of your disability and needs at its own expense.

You should expect your school to work with you in an interactive process to identify an appropriate academic adjustment. Unlike the experience you may have had in high school, however, do not expect your postsecondary school to invite your parents to participate in the process or to develop an IEP for you.

What if the academic adjustment we identified is not working? Let the school know as soon as you become aware that the results are not what you expected. It may be too late to correct the problem if you wait until the course or activity is completed. You and your school should work together to resolve the problem.

May a postsecondary school charge me for providing an academic adjustment? No. Furthermore, it may not charge students with disabilities more for participating in its programs or activities than it charges students who do not have disabilities.

What can I do if I believe the school is discriminating against me? Practically every postsecondary school must have a person— frequently called the Section 504 Coordinator, ADA Coordinator, or Disability Services Coordinator—who coordinates the school's compliance with Section 504 or Title II or both laws. You may contact this person for information about how to address your concerns.

The school must also have grievance procedures. These procedures are not the same as the due process procedures with which you may be familiar from high school. However, the postsecondary school's grievance procedures must include steps to ensure that you may raise your concerns fully and fairly and must provide for the prompt and equitable resolution of complaints.

School publications, such as student handbooks and catalogs, usually describe the steps you must take to start the grievance process. Often, schools have both formal and informal processes. If you decide to use a grievance process, you should be prepared to present all the reasons that support your request. . . .

Students Should Know Their Rights and Responsibilities

Students with disabilities who know their rights and responsibilities are much better equipped to succeed in postsecondary school. We encourage you to work with the staff at your school because they, too, want you to succeed. Seek the support of family, friends and fellow students, including those with disabilities. Know your talents and capitalize on them, and believe in yourself as you embrace new challenges in your education.

EIGHT

Girls Should Consider Nontraditional Careers

Green River Community College

> Green River Community College is a two-year public college in Washington State, offering degrees and certificates in academic and professional and technical programs, as well as courses in continuing education and developmental education. The following selection uses data from various sources to show how women are traditionally employed in much lower-paying jobs than men. According to the authors, women may improve their income potential by entering fields traditionally occupied by men.

The US Department of Labor defines a non-traditional field as one in which 25% or less of those individuals employed in that area are women. The School-to-Work Employment Act requires all states to have programs in place to prepare women for these fields and to help them be successful in them. This often includes many broad categories, such as math, science, and engineering, as well as occupations in construction trades, law enforcement, auto repair, welding, printing, truck driving, plumbing, computer maintenance and repair, and many other fields.

Fields Women Are Employees In

Only 14% of all working women are employed in non-traditional fields, the majority of which are blue collar or technical fields

Green River Community College Women's Programs, "About Non-Traditional Careers," April 4, 2006. Reproduced by permission.

that do not require a four-year college degree. The biggest gains in numbers of women in non-traditional fields recently have been in professional fields like engineering and law. For example, women engineering graduates went from about 1000 in 1977 to over 10,000 in 1997. Today, women earn close to 30% of all bachelor and master's degrees in engineering. However, fields that require less education are still struggling. Almost 1/4 of all working women are in clerical positions and approximately 1/5 are in service sector occupations.

About 54% of all working women are employed in low paying support jobs such as clerical workers, retail salespeople, waitresses and hairdressers. Women traditionally dominate these fields, but those women who work in non-traditional fields make 20–30% more than those who work in traditional fields. This kind of

Women who work in nontraditional career fields, such as carpentry, can make 20 to 30 percent more money than in the jobs women traditionally take.

occupational division has a huge impact on wages that women have the potential to earn, and many non-traditional fields can provide excellent salaries and benefits compared to "pink collar" fields that are dominated by women.

For example, starting wages for a childcare worker and a carpentry worker might be $7–$10 per hour. Once in an apprenticeship, a carpenter receives $12–$16 per hour. By the time the apprentice reaches a journey-level position, she could easily be making $35 per hour or more with excellent benefits. The childcare worker would probably have much more limited opportunities for paid training, wage advancement, benefits, and position progression.

Types of Nontraditional Jobs Women Take

Not all non-traditional jobs involve heavy labor. Many emerging fields, especially technology fields, offer great job prospects and wages without hard labor. For example, the Department of Labor projects that the computer field will generate 1 in 6 new jobs by the year 2005, but the number of women studying computer science is dropping. In 1984, women received 37% of all computer science degrees, but in ten years that percentage fell to 28%. In 2000, men with a B.A. earned $49,982 per year to a woman's $35,408 per year. Women with an M.A. earned almost $8000 a year less than a man with a B.A. does. . . .

Reasons Women Should Consider Nontraditional Jobs

- It is a fact that 54% of all working women are employed as clerical workers, retail salespersons, waitresses, and hairdressers, which can be classified as "traditional" female jobs or "pink collar" work
- Women in traditional jobs earn 20% to 30% less than women in non-traditional occupations. Such occupational segregation is the main reason why women make 76 cents for every dollar that men make nationally. . . .
- Many women are just as capable as men to meet the physical demands of non-traditional work

Nontraditional Occupations for Women, 2003 (numbers in thousands)

Occupation	Employed Both Sexes	Employed Females	Percent Female
Farmers and ranchers	825	204	24.7
Metalworkers and plastic workers	423	103	24.3
Detectives and criminal investigators	112	26	23.2
Chefs and head cooks	281	56	19.9
Industrial engineers, including health and safety	180	35	19.4
Barbers	95	17	17.9
Meter readers, utilities	50	8	16.0
Chemical engineers	75	11	14.7
Clergy	410	57	13.9
Taxi drivers and chauffeurs	286	39	13.6
Computer hardware engineers	99	10	10.1
Construction and building inspectors	95	9	9.5
Industrial truck and tractor operators	534	46	8.6
Broadcast and sound engineering technicians and radio operators	94	8	8.5
Painting, construction, and maintenance	660	44	6.7
Cabinet makers and bench carpenters	70	4	5.7
Firefighters	258	9	3.5
Aircraft pilots and flight engineers	116	4	3.4
Electricians	774	16	2.1
Carpenters	1,595	26	1.6

Taken from: U.S. Department of Labor. www.dol.gov/wb.

- Women who choose non-traditional work enjoy a high degree of work satisfaction
- Non-traditional jobs better enable women to support themselves and their families
- All workers, male and female, have a right to choose among a full range of occupations, not just those dictated by traditional expectations

A Self-Assessment for Women Considering a Nontraditional Career

Are you . . .

A person who likes to take on challenges?

In good physical health or physically fit?

A person who needs to earn more than $8.00 per hour to support yourself and your family?

A person who needs to have access to health care and other benefits?

Willing to explore new things, new places, and new people?

Have you . . .

Worked in a non-traditional job before as a paid worker, volunteer, or as a hobby?

Received a high school diploma or GED?

Obtained your driver's license?

Traveled and enjoyed going from place to place?

Used tools to build or repair items in your home or apartment?

Worked on your car or someone else's?

Done handiwork such as knitting or crafts?

Followed a pattern in sewing?

Regularly participated in a sport or a work out?

Planted and maintained a successful garden?

Fixed a broken television, radio, or computer?

Entered/completed a trade school program for a vocational skill?

Driven/fixed farm machinery?

Used power tools/built a piece of furniture?

Followed a recipe?

Worked independently, with little supervision?

Do you dislike . . .

Working at a desk all day?

Working with groups of children or sick people?

Dealing regularly with the public in a store or restaurant?

Helping others solve their personal or family problems?

Working indoors?

Working in one place all day?

Answering questions and referring people to other sources of information?

Completing written products?

Using the same equipment all the time?

Work in which you rarely use your physical strength?

Receiving lots of supervision and feedback on your work?

Do you like to . . .

Work with your hands?

Make repairs around the house?

Fix outlets, radios, and/or stereos?

Work outdoors?

Drive cars, vans, and/or farm equipment?

See concrete results from your work?

Solve technical problems or puzzles?

Work from a pattern, blueprint, or diagram to construct or make things?

Paint, wallpaper, and fill in holes in the walls?

NINE

The Military Offers Valuable Training for Civilian Careers

C. Hall Dillon

In the following viewpoint C. Hall Dillon, an economist in the Office of Occupational Statistics and Employment Projection, Bureau of Labor Statistics, highlights the career value of military service. The military has 140 occupational specialties, including aviation, health care, and law enforcement. Dillon points out that students can get formal training in some technical occupations during military service, receive a college degree through a variety of options, or apply for college credit equivalency for training received through the military.

Men and women serve in the U.S. Armed Forces for a variety of reasons. Some consider military service a matter of family tradition or patriotic duty. Others want to further their education or see the world. Still others seek the kind of character-building challenges that the armed services offer.

For many people, military service provides all of these things, and more: Another draw for prospective servicemembers is the chance to gain hands-on experience. The military trains people for numerous occupations that have civilian counterparts, such as air traffic controller, plumber, and paramedic. It may help their

C. Hall Dillon, "Military Training for Civilian Careers (or: How to Gain Practical Experience While Serving Your Country)," *Occupational Outlook Quarterly Online*/U.S. Department of Labor Bureau of Labor Statistics, Spring 2007.

job search later, too. In August 2005, the unemployment rate for veterans (3.9 percent) was slightly lower than the unemployment rate for the labor force as a whole (4.6 percent), according to data from the U.S. Bureau of Labor Statistics.

Joining the Armed Services Is a Commitment

But joining the armed services is a serious commitment. Signing a contract obliges service for a specified number of years—and, unlike other employers, the U.S. Armed Forces offer no option to walk away before that contractual period ends. And there's always the possibility of combat.

In other words, this high-quality training comes with some pretty strong strings attached. . . .

Many workers in aviation started their careers in the military as mechanics, air traffic controllers, and air crews.

Military Training Teaches More than an Occupation

The military trains you to be technically proficient in whatever occupation you are assigned. But you'll also learn teamwork, perseverance, leadership, and other skills widely applicable in the civilian workforce. In fact, some employers looking for workers with specific qualifications, such as security clearances, often seek out former military personnel.

Most armed-services jobs have a direct civilian counterpart. If you learn how to repair and maintain vehicles, for example, you might later use these skills as a mechanic in the civilian world. If you're trained to cook for a battalion, you could be well on your way to becoming a chef. And if you learn to maintain military computer systems, you might find civilian work as a computer specialist.

In the military, you'll earn career credentials. You'll also have a chance to further your education while you serve—and afterward.

Enlisted personnel fill more than four-fifths of the military jobs available. Officers, who are not the focus of this article, fill the remaining portion in jobs like nurse, pilot, and lawyer. . . .

The Military Has 140 Occupational Specialties

The military has more than 140 occupational specialties, most of which relate to civilian jobs. Not all of these are available in every branch of the military. Your preferences will be considered, but the specialty you are assigned will depend on your aptitude and the needs of the armed services at the time you enlist.

The following are some examples of military occupational specialties.

Aviation. Workers in aviation, including air traffic controllers, air crew, and mechanics, often get their start in the armed services. Most people earn licenses from the Federal Aviation Administration as part of their training—and those are licenses that they can later use as civilians.

Combat operations. Enlisted servicemembers in combat operations have jobs that are among the most specific to the military: infantry, armored vehicle operation, artillery and missile crew, and Special Forces. Although these specialties do not relate closely to civilian occupations, they teach skills that civilian employers value. Among the skills servicemembers learn are how to lead others, how to operate complex equipment, and how to perform under pressure.

Computers. Servicemembers in computer specialties learn to set up and troubleshoot computer networks and systems for the military. They also learn computer security: protecting computer systems from natural disasters and defending them from hackers and other threats. And some specialists earn widely accepted certifications. Computer specialists in the armed services are often prepared for civilian jobs as computer network and systems administrators, computer support technicians, and computer programmers.

Construction. To raise buildings and construct barricades and other structures, the military trains construction specialists. These servicemembers perform a range of tasks, including carpentry, plumbing, and masonry. They also train as cabinetmakers and surveying technicians. Some complete registered apprenticeships to become journeyworkers.

Food services. Fortunately for hungry service personnel, the military trains food service specialists to order, inspect, prepare, and serve healthy food. These specialists learn about many topics, including cooking methods, food storage, and, of course, cleanup. The skills are transferable to civilian jobs in restaurants, bakeries, hospitals, and other facilities that have their own food preparation services.

Healthcare. Healthcare practitioners and technicians of all types receive training in the military. Some do laboratory tests or provide dental care, for example, and others assist physical therapists or work as x-ray or other types of technicians. Still others perform tasks similar to those of paramedics and give medical care in emergencies and in the absence of doctors. Many healthcare workers learn more than one occupation. All are either partially or fully trained for civilian healthcare jobs.

Law enforcement. Many servicemembers train in police, security, and investigative jobs. Like civilian police, they learn

Many Jobs in the Armed Forces Have Civilian Counterparts

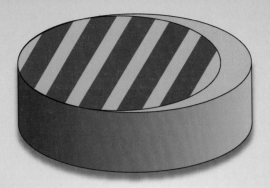

 Total jobs in the armed forces:
4,100

 Jobs in armed forces with civilian counterparts:
3,608

 Jobs in armed forces without civilian counterparts:
492

Eighty-eight percent of jobs in the armed forces have civilian counterparts.

Taken from: AllSchools.com, "Military Careers Statistics," 2006.

tasks such as collecting evidence, interviewing witnesses, and performing riot control. Servicemembers in this specialty are prepared for civilian jobs as police officers, security guards, and intelligence analysts.

Maintenance. In the armed services, people learn to fix all types of equipment. Automotive and heavy equipment repairers, for example, learn to fix cars and trucks, and they might also maintain tanks and bulldozers. Because of this wide-ranging experience, servicemembers trained in maintenance may qualify for complex civilian repair jobs.

Manufacturing and power plant operation. The military trains machinists, who create metal parts; welders; tool and die makers; and other manufacturing workers. And because the armed services need power for their bases and ships, they also train power plant electricians and power plant operators—who might later work in civilian power plants or as boiler operators.

Media and the arts. Training in media and the arts available to servicemembers includes graphic arts, broadcasting, and photography. The military's audio and broadcast technicians, for example, help to produce movies, television shows, and radio programs. The skills gained in these military jobs relate to civilian opportunities as commercial artists, musicians, and photojournalists, among others.

Becoming a Student in the Military

Perhaps you've heard that the military will pay for your college education, either in whole or in part, while you're serving and after—even retroactively. That's true; many of the same educational benefits that are available for veterans are offered to active-duty servicemembers and reservists. But you'll need to sort through the facts to learn how to become eligible.

Regardless of whether you go to college, however, you receive training and education while you serve.

If you join the military, you'll spend at least some time in a classroom. The subjects you take will depend on your occupational specialty. For example, quartermasters and boat operators receive instruction in navigational mathematics. Finance specialists learn bookkeeping and basic accounting. Pharmacy technicians are taught biology, chemistry, and the names and uses of medications.

This classroom instruction, plus on-the-job training, qualifies you for licenses, certifications, and college credit—all of which will be useful when you return to the civilian world as a jobseeker. Servicemembers in healthcare and aviation occupations, for example, often earn licenses required in civilian jobs, although they might need additional training.

Military Jobs with Formal Training

The military provides formal training in some technical occupations, including those in construction, manufacturing, and repair. Servicemembers who successfully complete registered apprenticeship programs earn a journeyworker certificate, recognized by civilian employers nationwide.

Also, armed-services class time and training are recognized by some professional associations as a way to qualify for occupational certifications. Each military branch offers servicemembers information about turning armed-services training into private certifications.

Classroom training could continue throughout your military career, as you gain expertise in your occupation or train for others. And your specialty might require new skills, such as speaking a foreign language, to prepare for a mission.

Turn Military Training into a College Degree

You might be able to turn your military training into a college degree. For example, the U.S. Air Force runs its own community college, where servicemembers can earn an associate degree; the Navy's Program for Afloat College Education provides instruction for sailors at sea.

Attending a local civilian college or university might be another option. And the proliferation of online instruction and distance learning has broadened the possibilities for servicemembers stationed all over the world.

You might be able to get college credit without taking additional courses, based on your armed-services experience. Some servicemembers take equivalency exams to get college credit for what they've learned on the job. Others receive credit based on recommendations from the American Council on Education, an organization that certifies qualified training as equivalent to college coursework.

Other education benefits for active-duty servicemembers include tuition assistance, scholarships, loans, and grants for vocational and college training during or after service.

In addition, each military branch offers its own education benefits for career development. If it's important to you to get an education while you're in the service, be sure to compare programs when choosing a branch for enlistment.

Choosing and Joining a Military Branch

Deciding to pursue career training in the U.S. Armed Forces is the first of many steps to becoming a soldier, airman, sailor, Marine, or Coast Guardsman. There is also the decision about which branch to join. The armed services' five branches have a lot in common, but each has its own purpose. You'll need to learn what distinguishes each branch and whether it provides the kinds of opportunities you seek.

Do your research, take a few tests, and you might be ready to sign on the duty-bound line.

To learn about the armed services and the types of jobs they offer, get input from several sources. Study written material, watch video presentations, and talk to recruiters, family, and friends. Then, analyze the facts you've gathered to make an informed decision.

A good starting point is to look at each branch of service separately. Knowing more about what each does can help you to narrow your occupational focus.

The Army, Air Force, Navy, and Marine Corps fall under the U.S. Department of Defense. They provide the military forces needed to conduct or deter war and protect the Nation's security. The Coast Guard is part of the U.S. Department of Homeland Security and has a primarily domestic role in enforcing maritime law and safety.

Facts About the Branches

The Army is the largest of the five branches, with about 488,000 officers and enlisted soldiers on active duty. These personnel defend U.S. land and interests through ground-based operations in dozens of countries.

The Air Force, originally created as a ground-support corps of the Army, has roughly 347,000 active-duty personnel. They defend the Nation from the air and from space, operating and controlling aircraft, satellites, and missiles.

The role of the Navy is to maintain freedom of the seas. In addition to enabling trade and travel for the United States and its allies, a strong navy can use the oceans during times of conflict.

About 342,000 active-duty Navy personnel serve on ships, submarines, aircraft, and bases around the world.

The Marine Corps, part of the Department of the Navy, is the only branch of the armed services with air-, land-, and sea-based expeditionary fighting capabilities. Marines, who number around 178,000 on active duty, are trained to deploy quickly into situations ranging from peacekeeping to combat; they also guard U.S. embassies worldwide.

During peacetime, the Coast Guard focuses on maritime rescue, safety, law enforcement, and border control. In times of conflict, the President—the Commander in Chief—can transfer all or some of the 38,000 active-duty members of the Coast Guard to the Department of the Navy.

Remember, there is some overlap between the branches' functions. The Air Force might seem an obvious choice for jobs related to airplanes, for example, but all five branches have aircraft-related occupations. Thoroughly investigate your options if you want to train for a particular job.

Acquiring Recruitment Information

Military recruitment information exists in many forms: posters and brochures, Web-based videos and written materials, and radio and television spots. But information also comes from talking with other people, including current and former military personnel and recruiters for each of the branches.

Some information for making comparisons is easy to find. For example, each branch provides details about its education benefits and eligibility requirements. You can compare those details to help you decide which branch to join—or not join.

When evaluating the materials you read, see, or hear, however, keep in mind that their purpose is to promote the armed services. You might find the occupational profiles for one branch appealing, but don't be too quick to disregard the other branches in the beginning.

A major part of your decisionmaking process should involve talking to others. Current and former servicemembers can tell you about their active-duty job, which is especially helpful if it's the type of work you'd like to do. But remember that each person's military experience, positive or negative, is filtered through a different prism.

Meeting with Recruiters

This advice can also come from recruiters, whose job is to tell you about the military in general and their branches in particular. Get the facts you need by asking specific questions about the occupational options in each branch, especially if you have a certain job in mind. Recruiters can also provide information about details such as signing bonuses, length of basic training, specifics about leave and medical care, conditions of living quarters, and details of education benefits.

For balance, talk to more than one recruiter from each branch. Be informed enough to ask specifically about topics, such as options for joining the Reserves, that the recruiter might not mention otherwise. And trust your instincts. Be wary of any recruiter whom you feel avoids directly responding to your questions.

The flipside to asking questions, of course, is listening to the answers. Consider bringing along a friend or family member to sit in on the session with you. Afterward, you can compare notes. Be aware, though, that the recruiter might ask personal questions. Make sure you don't mind that the person accompanying you will hear your answers to those questions.

TEN

Turning a Hobby into a Career

Olivia Crosby

In the following viewpoint Olivia Crosby, a contributing editor to *Occupational Outlook Quarterly*, examines a variety of hobbies that have the potential to become careers. She interviews numerous people in several different sectors, including a craft artist, a furniture maker, a sculptor, dog trainers, and a river guide. She also gives tips on how to use creative thinking to turn hobbies into careers. She points out that, even if a hobby does not lead directly to a career, it reveals skills, interests, and abilities that could help a job-seeker focus his or her search and find a satisfying career.

Imagine being paid for having fun. Many people make that dream a reality by finding a career related to their hobbies. Some turn their pastimes into paychecks, selling what they once made or did only in their free time. Others find jobs that use hobby-related skills or are related to their hobbies in another way. . . .

Consider an Arts Career

When he was in high school, Hayne Bayless spent every free period in the art room. Now, he makes his living as a potter in

Olivia Crosby, "From Hobby to Career: Transforming Your Pastime into a Profession," *Occupational Outlook Quarterly*/U.S. Department of Labor, Bureau of Labor Statistics, Fall 2001.

Ivoryton, Connecticut, selling his creations at craftshows and galleries across the country.

The day-to-day work of a craft artist depends on the craft. Some artists work with glass, cutting and soldering stained glass or heating and shaping it into sculpture. Others work with fabric, weaving rugs and other textiles or designing and sewing clothes. Still others make jewelry or metal artwork. In fact, craft artists make nearly every type of handmade product, from ink stamps to baskets to papier mache.

Bayless spends most days in his studio creating pots and other clay vessels. His first step in making pottery is to sketch a rough picture of the piece he wants to make. But he stands ready to change his plans if new ideas strike as he works. Using a process called handbuilding, Bayless sculpts each piece of pottery. He rolls the clay into slabs, then cuts, molds, and bends it into shape and adds texture. He smoothes separate parts together until he has the shape he wants. Then, he puts the piece on a shelf to dry and fires it in a hot oven, called a kiln. After the firing, Bayless paints the pottery with a glaze made of chemicals he mixes to give the piece color and texture. He completes the piece by firing it a second time.

Darlys Ewoldt, a metalworker in Chicago, also spends most of each day creating art. She, too, starts with a rough sketch of the piece she wants to make. After drawing her design, she hammers sections of metal into shape. When she is satisfied with the metal's form, she paints it with chemicals to change its color. Just as potters experiment with new glazes, Ewoldt experiments to see how different chemicals react to various metals.

Furniture maker Craig Stevens prepares more detailed plans than potters and metalworkers do before starting a piece. Stevens, who works in his shop in Sunbury, Ohio, often creates furniture to fit a specific space in customers' homes. He carefully drafts each part of the piece on graph paper and meets with customers to perfect his concept. Then, he uses woodworking tools to saw, shape, and carve the wood. Each step in Stevens' work builds on earlier steps, so he needs to plan far in advance. In a final and favorite step, Stevens adds carvings and finishes to the furniture surfaces. . . .

Selling Crafts

An important part of professional crafting is finding a way to sell one's creations. Art and craft shows provide a forum for crafters to display their wares and explain their work to potential customers. Most craft artists research shows to decide which to exhibit in and then apply to the best by filling out forms. In addition to describing their pieces and work process, craft artists submit several photographs of their work with each application. Ewoldt photographs her own sculpture because she learned the technique in art school. But many craft artists hire a product photographer to take application photos for them.

Ewoldt, Bayless, and Stevens attend two to five shows a year. But most craft artists attend more, especially those whose work is less expensive or takes less time to make. Until recently, Christine Casey, who makes clay ornaments in Acton, Massachusetts, applied and traveled to more than 50 shows every year. Many were far from home. "I was on the road 30 weekends a year," she says. Casey now attends fewer shows because she receives orders at her studio from several wholesalers she met at previous shows. Those wholesalers sell her work to retail stores. And, like many craft artists, Casey also receives orders through a website she maintains.

Craft artists also sell their work in craft malls and art galleries. This kind of selling requires its own preparation. Craft artists search for galleries that attract customers who would be interested in their work. Then, they apply to the gallery by sending photos of their work with a letter of introduction. If the work sells, the artist receives a percentage of the selling price. . . .

Becoming a Craft Artist

Becoming a craft artist requires mastery of a craft, and there are several ways to accomplish this. Many craft artists get a formal education in the arts. Ewoldt, for instance, earned a master's degree in fine arts before she began her career. Stevens earned a bachelor's degree in art and attended an expert woodworking school.

Some craft artists learn their trade in workshops and short-term classes while they maintain other jobs. Bayless is one example.

He started making pottery in high school but never studied it in college. Only after earning a degree in journalism and writing for a newspaper did he begin to take classes at a local art school.

Other artists learn primarily by practice. Casey started making ornaments for family and friends. Before she started selling them, she perfected her technique by reading instruction books and experimenting.

Working with a more experienced craft artist is another good way to learn. "It is very helpful to study with an expert before starting on your own," says Ewoldt, who completed a 2-year apprenticeship with a commercial jewelrymaker before selling her own creations. Apprenticeships not only teach craft artists new crafting skills, they also expose artists to the business aspects of selling crafts. There are plenty of apprenticeship opportunities; more than 16 percent of craft artists hire assistants, according to the Craft Organizations Directors' study.

Part of the business preparation craft artists need is learning how to record income and expenses and to set prices. "The most successful people research the market before they start," says Casey. "They visit craftshows and artshops and giftshops to see what prices other people charge. Then, they figure out how much time and money it takes to make their pieces."

Most artists begin by selling their work at small, community-based shows. Later, they apply to juried shows and offer their work to local galleries. . . .

Pet Owner to Pet Trainer

Matthew Margolis' family owned four dogs while he was growing up. Taking care of them was his favorite pastime. Today, he owns a training business in Los Angeles, hosts a dog training television show, and teaches others how to train. "I've always loved animals," he says, "and I made my passion my profession."

Barbara Giella, a dog trainer and behavior counselor in New York City, also found her career through love of a pet. She changed occupations from college professor to dog trainer after learning to train her puppy. She teaches dogs to be good

Median Annual Income for Various Jobs

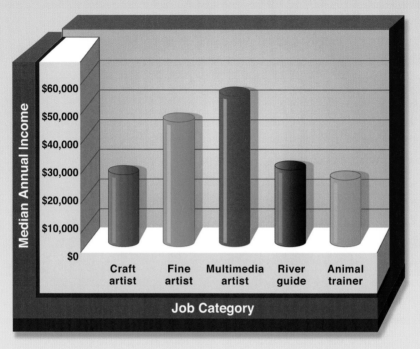

Taken from: Olivia Crosby, "From Hobby to Career: Transforming Your Pastime into a Profession," *Occupational Outlook Quarterly Online* (Fall 2001), for river guide. All others from: U.S. Department of Labor, Bureau of Labor Statistics, 2008–2009 Report. www.bls.gov/oco.

companions. Trainers instruct dogs to respond to commands. In the process, they turn dogs into mannerly housemates and teach them to stop dangerous or annoying activities, such as chasing cars or stealing food.

Giella and Margolis, like many trainers, go to owners' homes for private consultations. They often are asked to solve specific problems: climbing onto furniture, biting, and jumping on people are some examples. "We find out why the dog is behaving that way so we can change the behavior," says Giella. "Dogs have to be taught how to live with people. It doesn't come naturally." In-house training also helps dogs with territorial issues. One of Giella's more challenging problems is helping people raise puppies in cramped city apartments. . . .

Requirements for a Dog Trainer

Dog trainers need to be patient and resourceful. Instead of becoming frustrated with dogs or owners, they must find new ways of teaching and communicating. And good trainers are observant, able to read a dog's body language.

Trainers also need to be physically fit to run and walk with dogs, but they do not need herculean power. "Training is about technique," says Giella, "not strength."

Good interpersonal skills are also important, especially when trainers are teaching dog owners. Many trainers can hone interpersonal and public speaking skills on the job.

Becoming a Dog Trainer

Nearly all pet dog trainers get their start by training their own dogs or joining animal-care groups such as 4-H. To gain professional skills, dog trainers attend workshops presented by expert trainers and animal behaviorists. Dog trainers usually attend at least 24 seminars before training professionally.

Some trainers take courses in animal learning and behavior at colleges and universities. This gives them a thorough understanding of the theories behind dog training. Trainers also can learn by reading books and watching videotapes. But before they can instruct professionally, they need hands-on experience.

Many prospective trainers complete a formal program of study at a training school. Students need to be careful when choosing a school. There are no formal standards or accreditation systems in pet training, so it can be difficult to judge a school's quality. Veterinarians, animal shelters, humane societies, dog owners' clubs, and dog trainer associations often can recommend good courses.

Apprenticing with an experienced trainer is another good way to learn. But again, students must be cautious. "Many people set themselves up as teachers, but they don't know effective and humane technique," says Margolis. "Check credentials and methods."

Finally, some trainers prepare on the job. They learn to train after being hired by a training company, pet store, or pet-supply store. New employees take company-provided classes for several weeks or months. Then, they start as assistant trainers before working independently.

Preparation for assistance-dog trainers usually involves completion of education programs at the organizations in which they will work. Most assistance-dog training organizations offer their own preparation so that dog trainers learn their methods.

Entry-level positions at assistance-dog organizations are highly competitive. Applicants most likely to be hired have excellent communication skills, experience with animals, and experience helping people with disabilities. "I look for people who love dogs," says [trainer Jo] Pfaff. "But working well with people is even more important." Nonetheless, she says that training pets and raising puppies for an assistance-dog organization are good ways to prepare. . . .

Sports Enthusiast to River Guide

Bettina George used to paddle boats on the weekends and teach elementary school on the weekdays. But after taking boating classes in the summers, she made boating her full-time job. Today, she teaches kayaking and guides rafts for the Nantahala Outdoor Center in Mountain Rest, South Carolina.

River guides lead groups of boaters down rivers. They choose a safe route down the water and teach their passengers how to paddle. River guides make paddling rivers look easy, but it can be a challenge. Guides must read the water, looking for frothy eddies, rocks that affect currents, and moving debris.

Guides' work starts before boaters arrive. Each morning, they pack supplies and boats and load the vans that will take them to the river. They observe weather conditions and water levels to decide which trips will go forward. Most guides paddle rivers that have already been scouted, but they still need to check their routes for hazards.

When boaters arrive, guides teach them basic strokes. In rafts, passengers learn how and when to move from one side of the raft to the other, shifting its weight to maintain balance. After everyone dons a life jacket, the trip begins.

Whitewater trips are the most exciting for guides. But they also require the most care. As George says, "Lots of people fall out of the raft." When that happens, guides fish them out by their lifejackets or throw them a rope.

Skills Required to Be a River Guide

During any kind of trip, guides have to be alert for changing river conditions. "On long trips, there's no turning back when there's trouble," says Vitchai Cain, a guide formerly with Big Bend River in Terlingua, Texas. "You have to deal with whatever happens." That could mean contending with medical emergencies or unruly passengers.

In addition to navigating rivers, guides entertain their passengers. They explain the history of the area and point out animals and plants that live along the river route.

Many guides, including Cain, lead trips that include overnight stops. As dusk falls, Cain guides the boats to a campsite and sets up camp for the night. While the passengers relax, he and his fellow guide start cooking dinner. "People are amazed at what we can make out there," says Cain. His specialties include lasagna, enchiladas, and chocolate cake. He makes sure his passengers are happy and having fun around the campfire. . . .

Characteristics of a River Guide

All guides need well-developed paddling skills. Sometimes, boaters with rudimentary skills can start as entertainers aboard rafts while they are improving their boating ability. Guides also need to be calm and clearheaded under pressure.

Strength is another asset for guides, although the best guides substitute technique for brute force. "If you're good," explains Cain, "you don't need to make last-minute corrections. Corrections are what take real strength."

Guides also need to be competent leaders, particularly if they lead whitewater or sea kayaking trips. They should inspire confidence and help passengers understand and follow instructions. Diplomacy and an outgoing personality also are needed to make trips fun, which is especially important for trips involving children or overnight jaunts.

Becoming a River Guide

Nearly all guides need CPR [cardiopulmonary resuscitation] certification. Most also complete safety training, in Wilderness First Aid or as Wilderness First Responders or Wilderness Emergency Medical Technicians, through one of several commercial schools. This supplemental training teaches them to assess and stabilize injured or sick boaters in areas where doctors are not available. People with standard emergency medical technician or first responder credentials can earn wilderness certification by completing a wilderness transition course.

Many guides also need training as swift water rescue technicians. They learn how to swim in whitewater and how to use ropes to rescue boaters from water.

Several States require guides to become licensed before guiding a boat independently. In most of these States, requirements include proof of employment at a licensed rafting company and completion of courses in first aid.

Before they lead trips, all guides complete their rafting companies' training programs. First, they ride in a guided raft. Then, they guide an empty raft down the river. Finally, they assist experienced guides many times before guiding alone. Each river is different, so workers have to train on every river they will guide.

Guides also need to learn the ecology and physical and cultural history of the river they travel. Some learn this on the job. But others have formal education in these subjects. Cain, for instance, has a bachelor's degree in geology—training he says he uses to explain rock formations along the river.

Those who want to teach paddling can earn certification from the American Canoeing Association. The association offers certification for teachers of rafting, canoeing, river kayaking, sea kayaking, and swift water rescue. It also certifies teachers in adaptation techniques for boaters who are disabled. Each certification requires classes at an approved school and a passing score on a certification exam. . . .

Capitalizing on Your Sideline

Finding a job centered on a hobby often takes creative thinking, but it can be done. Many jobs use hobbyists' expertise. Here are a few of the common ways in which favorite bailiwicks become wageworthy.

Selling what you do or make. Many people earn money selling their activity or its results. You can do this by working in an established business or by starting your own enterprise. If you start your own business, be ready for entrepreneurial tasks, including accounting, market research, and employee management. And arm yourself for success by writing a business plan describing your target customers, your projected income and expenses, and your startup costs, among other things. You will need to research and follow zoning, income tax, and sales tax laws and register your business with your State and county governments.

Teaching the hobby. Another option is to teach others about the pastime you like. You might teach at a school, either as an elementary, high school, or university instructor, or as an enrichment teacher in a community center or college. Many hobby supply stores also have opportunities for teachers. Music stores and fabric stores, for example, often pay experts to teach customers new skills.

Selling or promoting hobby equipment. Most hobbies require supplies—potting soil, birdseed, guitar picks, and other equipment. Workers sell those supplies and advise customers on which to choose and how to use them. Some companies also hire enthusiasts part time to promote hobby equipment at trade shows and competitions.

More Ways to Turn Hobbies into Careers

Repairing hobby equipment. From bicycle shops to violin repair studios, many businesses keep hobby equipment in working order. And being skilled in the hobby is usually a prerequisite for store workers.

Hobby communications. Your expertise could turn into a writing or visual arts career. Many hobbies have trade magazines written for aficionados. These magazines need article writers and editors. Magazines also need photographs and illustrations, which they may buy from stock suppliers. Specialty areas, such as food photography and wildlife illustration, also require skilled artists. Other visual arts opportunities include videography, such as filming people performing a sport.

Hobby organizations. Some hobbyists have associations to promote their activities and share ideas. Workers in these organizations keep membership lists, arrange meetings, coordinate educational programs, and promote the group's ideas. Finding paid jobs in these organizations is difficult because many hobby associations are small or are managed by volunteers. But a few paid jobs exist, and workers who have them are at the forefront of their hobbies' developments.

Many animal lovers seek careers in animal training, care, and veterinary medicine.

Connecting Pastimes to Occupations

Even if you don't have a job centered on a particular hobby, you can still use your interests to find a career. Hobbies provide information about the skills you like using—skills that can be applied to several occupations.

To find an occupation related to your hobby interests, first decide which hobby-related skills you enjoy most. Occupations that use favorite abilities are probably the ones that suit you best. Dental technicians, for example, use sculpting and colorist skills to mold dentures and paint them to look realistic.

Identifying other interests is another important step because most occupations require many different types of skills. Coupling an interest in people with an interest in sports, for example, could lead to a job as a recreational therapist. Or if you enjoy science as well as pet care, a job as a veterinarian or biologist might agree with you. . . .

Resources Beyond Hobbies

Learn more about how your interests relate to careers by visiting a career or guidance counselor. You might take a career interest inventory to see how the activities you like compare with those preferred by workers in different types of jobs. And because interests are only part of choosing a career, counselors also might discuss your other job-related characteristics, including work and volunteer experiences, favorite classes and projects, hopes for future earnings, and educational plans.

Many career guidance books also can help you learn about careers and how they relate to your interests.

ELEVEN

Internships Help Students Learn Valuable Career Skills

Beth Mirza

In the following viewpoint, Beth Mirza outlines the advantages of internships in preparing students for the workforce. The author focuses on a specific program called the Mayor's Youth Program, which matches Atlanta public high school graduates with paid internships in the metropolitan region. Although at first most students were unprepared for the office, with some extra training they improved and gained valuable skills and experience they can use as a stepping-stone in their career. Mirza is senior editor for *HR News*.

For the past three years [since 2005], Atlanta Mayor Shirley Franklin has sponsored a program matching Atlanta public high school graduates with paid internships in the metropolitan region. Called the Mayor's Youth Program, the initiative gives the teens money for living expenses they'll incur as they move on to post-secondary education. And the teens gain "real world" work experience.

Unfortunately, some participating employers reported back to the Mayor's Youth Program that the students weren't ready for office life yet.

Beth Mirza, "Getting Ready for the World of Work: SHRM-Atlanta Prepares Students for Internships," *HRMagazine*, v. 53, February 2008, p. 92. Copyright © Society for Human Resource Management, 2008. Reproduced by permission.

Most Students Are Unprepared for the Workplace

"In our first years, as students were being placed in their summer internships, [we] did not take into account that some of our student participants have never held a job before, or certainly not in the public arena," said Gabrielle Allmon, coordinator for the Mayor's Youth Program at the Atlanta Workforce Development Agency, which helps administer the program. "As a result, some of our students were unaware of the do's and don'ts of the workplace."

In 2006, Suzanne LaVoy and Anne Dittman were co-vice-presidents of special events for SHRM [Society for Human Resource Management]-Atlanta. Lavoy, director of marketing for

A high school student receives advice as part of her internship at a landscape architecture firm.

Talent Connections in Roswell, Ga., heard Franklin speak about the internship project in 2006. She and Dittman, director of global business development for TRC Global Solutions in the Atlanta region, offered on behalf of the chapter to partner with the city of Atlanta to help the students learn workplace skills and adapt to business culture.

In the spring of 2007, SHRM-Atlanta's HR [human resources] professionals introduced time management, communications, ethics, dressing for the workplace, budgeting and finances to more than 700 high school seniors, Dittman said. The volunteers developed the curriculum for the courses, taught the classes at six Saturday sessions, and prepared binders and classroom materials.

In the fall, the city asked SHRM-Atlanta to interview hundreds of teens applying to be in the Mayor's Youth Program and assess whether the students were ready to tackle workforce challenges. The teens were interviewed as they waited to speak one-on-one with the mayor about their educational and professional goals.

As a result of the spring courses, "employers gave really positive feedback of the students' professionalism and work ethic," Allmon said. "The Mayor's Youth Program attributes much of the success of the 2007 summer internship session to the skills training SHRM-Atlanta provided the students."

And in December 2007, the American Society of Association Executives (ASAE) & The Center for Association Leadership gave SHRM-Atlanta an Award of Excellence in the 2008 Associations Advance America Awards.

SHRM-Atlanta's partnership with the Mayor's Youth Program has been a labor of love for everyone involved, LaVoy said.

"This is why [the volunteers] went into HR to start with," she said. "It fits with what they want to do in life."

Acquiring Skills for the Business World

Each Saturday, a new group of students sat for the courses led by two SHRM-Atlanta HR professionals.

Sherrie Maxwell, a consultant, helped teach the budget and finance and "dressing for success" courses. Students were asked to list all the times they spent money in the course of a month.

Tallying their income and expenses, Maxwell helped them create sample budgets—and get an idea of how to live within their means when they start college.

Lisa Goodman, vice president of HR at TRX Inc., helped teach the ethics course. The instructors and students talked about what unethical behavior is. They role-played ethical decision-making, she said, and used scenarios that students would be familiar with, such as downloading music from the Internet without paying for it.

For the time management courses, Kat Cole, vice president of training and development for Hooters of America, updated the curriculum that the city of Atlanta had previously given to the students by adding Hooters' own training. Patricia Kellner, SPHR, HR manager at Hooters, also helped teach the class.

In the workplace today, Cole said, new workers "pull out cell phones [while interacting with a customer], chew gum, show up late and take long breaks. Those are things that would keep [students] from having or keeping a job.

"It's not correct behavior, and they knew it wasn't correct, but they hadn't thought through the consequences," Cole added.

The Interview Process

The volunteers also coached the students on communication during the fall interviews.

"Teens talk slang; they aren't using plain English to say what they mean," said Maxwell, who encouraged the teens to record themselves as they spoke, then listen to how others hear them.

After the interview, the volunteers gave the students pointers on areas in which they needed to improve, such as eye contact, shaking hands, and showing a passion to be a part of the program.

Without those communication skills, employers might miss out on all the students have to offer.

"These are kids who are getting good grades, going to college, have part-time jobs and do extracurricular activities," Kellner said.

"They were not there with their hands open," agreed Tina Spencer, director of HR at Ivan Allen Workplace. Spencer helped teach the budgeting and finance courses and organize the fall interviews. "They . . . are in student body congresses and in sports. They have a grip on what they need to do to get to the next step."

Students Are Better Equipped to Enter the Workforce

According to Allmon, approximately 93 percent of the Mayor's Youth Program participants go on to some kind of post-secondary education. Because the program started in 2005, "we will have to wait until May 2009 to see the true success of this program in [college] graduation rates," she said.

The mayor started the program because "the [high school] dropout rate was up and the graduation rate was down," Allmon said. "She couldn't watch this happen in her own backyard, so she 'adopted' the senior class of the Atlanta Public Schools and assured them she would do her best to help everyone devise a plan for after high school. Everyone doesn't have to have the same plan, but they do need to have a plan."

Franklin's term ends in 2009, Allmon said, but she is working to set up an endowment so that the program can continue after her time in office.

SHRM-Atlanta is preparing for the spring, when volunteers will again teach the courses to the students in the Mayor's Youth Program. Though it's hard work, chapter members said they are reaping personal benefits—and professional benefits, too.

"These young people are about to break into the age where they'll get an entry-level job," said Cole. "On our behalf, it's good to mention our brand [Hooters], and they giggle and think that's cool or funny. But it's also serious, to have people stand up and say there are other jobs available in the restaurant industry," jobs that don't involve cooking or waiting tables.

At the end of the day, "I was exhausted and my feet hurt," Goodman said. "But I felt that if I had impacted one participant's personal or professional growth, it was worth it. This is going to be the workforce we're going to need down the road."

TWELVE

Apprenticeships and Careers in the Trades

EM Guild, Inc.

> In the following viewpoint the authors outline the advantages of learning a trade instead of going to college. They quote the National Association of Manufacturers as indicating there will be 10 million new workers required in the next decade in manufacturing. The authors profile workers in four different trades—an electrician, a diesel mechanic, a sheet metal worker, and a construction manager—outlining the education requirements, salary, on-the-job details, and the rewards and challenges of each job.

With tuitions rising and the trades and military actively seeking talented young people, many graduates are not taking a direct route to a higher education. Of the 2.5 million high school students who graduated in 2001, only about 60 percent headed off to college the next fall, according to a recent study by the Bureau of Labor Statistics.

Advantages of Learning a Trade

"Also, when you learn a trade, instead of paying money out toward college you can be bringing money in," says A. J. Pearson, executive director of the National Joint Apprenticeship and Training Committee. Apprentices in the field of electrical contracting earn

"Careers in the Trades," *Careers & Colleges*, vol. 24, pp. 40–43. Reproduced by permission.

After completing a five-year apprenticeship program, this electrician can look forward to a career earning him from sixty thousand to seventy thousand dollars per year.

about $8 to $9 an hour while they are learning the trade. After completing a five-year apprenticeship, an electrical contractor can be earning as high as $60,000 to $70,000 a year.

"People have a misconception that this is just common, dirty work," says Pearson. "But there's a very technical aspect that requires a knowledge of basic algebra, and there's a pride in the craftsmanship required of this work."

The National Association of Manufacturers (NAM) is another group that is actively recruiting. "In the next decade, 10 million new workers will be needed in manufacturing," says Wade Sayer, director of business education programs for NAM. "Manufacturing means everything from making potato chips to making computer chips, and opportunities range from tool-and-die work to advanced robotics. Plus many manufacturers give tuition reimbursement to learn on the job." . . .

Electrician Tayika S. Shaw

Age: 26

Location: Lubbock, TX

Job: Journeyman Electrician, J&T Shaw Electric.

Education: Shaw completed a five-year earn-and-learn apprenticeship program through the National Joint Apprenticeship Training Committee (NJATC). Shaw worked 40 hours a week learning the trade while going to classes two nights a week.

Salary: According to Salary.com, the national median salary is $39,764.

Starting out: As a child, Shaw was fascinated watching her uncle tinker with electronic gadgets. In her senior year at Palo Verde High School in Tucson, she decided to take a basic electrical wiring class. Her instructor turned her on to the career and told her about the apprenticeship program.

On the job: Shaw and her husband (whom she met during her on-the-job training) have their own electric company, servicing local residences and businesses. Sometimes she's doing repairs, installing electrical service, or wiring appliances. As one of the few female electricians in the industry and the first African-American woman to have completed the training program in Lubbock, Shaw often gets surprised reactions when she's on the job. "But then people will come up and say they're inspired," she says. "Sometimes women even ask me how they can get into the field." A big part of the job is trouble-shooting. She remembers fixing a restaurant fryer, an appliance she wasn't familiar with. "There are so many little wires. You just have to relax, think about your training, and start doing a process of elimination to see where the trouble is." On a typical day she uses screwdrivers, pliers, nut drivers, levels, measuring tape, a cordless drill, and a ladder. The job can also be physically demanding (climbing up and down ladders) and sometimes dirty (doing underground electrical work in ditches).

Rewards: "The awesome thing is that once you complete the [apprenticeship] program, you get your 'journeyman's ticket,' which allows you to work for different unions across the country at a great salary."

Challenges: "I have a big phobia of bugs. Sometimes we go in a crawl space, and there are bugs, rodents, or dead cats. That's when the girl in me comes out." . . .

Diesel Mechanic Matt Riello

Age: 35

Location: Union, NJ

Job: Diesel instructor at Engine City Technical Institute.

Education: To become a diesel mechanic/technician, you typically must complete a certification program that takes about 11 months.

Salary: Certified diesel mechanics start at about $30,000 to $35,000 a year; Class A mechanics can earn as much as $70,000 a year.

Starting out: In high school, Riello always wanted to be an auto mechanic, but he decided to go to college and earned a bachelor's in industrial engineering from Trenton State College in New Jersey. When he graduated, he worked for hazardous waste treatment facilities. "I found the corporate environment to be kind of a drag and very stressful," says Riello. "I wasn't doing hands-on work and I was really missing that." That's when he decided to pursue training at Engine City. Soon he was working on diesel engines for Ryder, the truck rental company, and Caterpillar, the heavy equipment manufacturer. Today, Riello teaches others how to be mechanics. "This is not a career for dummies," advises Riello. "You need to keep up with your math and reading skills because the job is becoming technically advanced."

On the job: Riello teaches students how to diagnose, repair, and completely overhaul truck engines, marine engines, and power generators. He conducts sessions on fixing electrical systems, accessories, and brake systems. He stresses that this field has become increasingly sophisticated as trucks rely on onboard computers that monitor engine performance and tell them how to run. His class of about 20 students learns by working on real repairs. "Plus, they fill our repair orders, talk with suppliers, and use all the hand tools needed for the job," says Riello.

Rewards: "Diagnosing and repairing engines is a lot like being a doctor. Engines are like people, and you really have to listen to them. It's the greatest satisfaction to get a truck back in shape and see the results of your work."

Challenges: "You have to be sharp and fast to keep up with the work load, but it really just takes some ambition. This career is very physical and you'll develop big forearms from all the wrench work." . . .

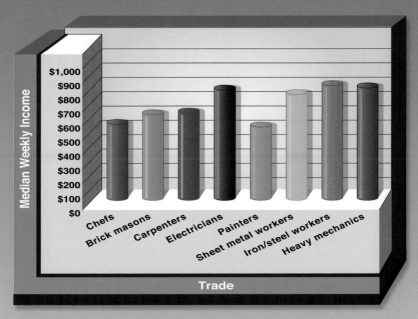

Median Weekly Incomes for Workers of Both Sexes in the Trades

Trades: Chefs, Brick masons, Carpenters, Electricians, Painters, Sheet metal workers, Iron/steel workers, Heavy mechanics

Median Weekly Income axis: $0, $100, $200, $300, $400, $500, $600, $700, $800, $900, $1,000

Taken from: U.S. Department of Labor, Bureau of Labor Statistics, "Median Weekly Earnings of Full-Time Wage and Salary Workers by Detailed Occupation," 2006. www.bls.gov.

Sheet Metal Worker Michael Smith

Age: 27

Location: Cudahy, WI

Job: Architectural sheet metal apprentice.

Education: These professionals must complete an apprenticeship, typically lasting four or five years. Smith has training in drafting, welding, and shop fabrication (processing materials to the specifications of a particular project in the shop).

Salary: Median hourly salary is $15.31 per hour.

Starting out: Smith first thought he might pursue a career as an architect, but he wanted to earn cash more quickly and decided that by working as a sheet metal apprentice he could earn a living while learning a trade.

On the job: As an apprentice providing general roofing services to many commercial buildings, Smith knows people in high places and has worked on high-profile jobs like the Milwaukee Art Museum and a local football stadium. Basically, he measures, cuts, and installs metal roofing panels using hand tools, power tools, machines, and heavy equipment. The apprentice reads and interprets blueprints or sketches to determine the method for fabricating, assembling and installing sheet metal products, such as copper, steel, iron, aluminum, or even non-metals such as plastic or fiberglass. "The job involves a lot of math," says Smith, "measuring surface areas, lengths, and angles."

Rewards: "It's satisfying to take raw material and make something useful out of it. Plus, the job is very secure and you know you're going to advance financially as you advance as an apprentice and on to journeyman status."

Challenges: "This is very physical work but I enjoy working with my hands." . . .

Construction Manager Caine Dearman

Age: 27

Location: Napa, CA

Job: Assistant project manager for NOVA Group Inc., a large general engineering contractor that specializes in building projects for the federal government.

Education: Some construction managers work their way up without a college degree by collecting years of experience in a trade. However; increasingly the trades are looking for people with college degrees in engineering, architecture, or construction management. Dearman earned a bachelor's in business from the University of Mississippi and a second bachelor's in construction management from the University of Southern Mississippi.

Salary: According to Dearman, assistant project managers may start at $35,000 to $45,000. Project managers may earn anywhere from $60,000 to $150,000.

Starting out: When Dearman was a teen, his dad—also in the construction industry—gave him summer jobs doing hard construction labor, such as digging ditches and pushing heavy wheelbarrow loads. The exhausting work convinced Dearman that he loved the industry but would want to get his college degree so he could get into management quickly. At the University of Southern Mississippi, Dearman was part of a five-person team that competed in ABC's [Association of Builders and Contractors] student construction management competition, where teams have six hours to draw up an estimate, schedule, and safety plan on a building project. At the competition he was recruited by NOVA and eventually got a job offer.

On the job: Most of NOVA Group's construction projects are located on military bases on the West Coast and in places like Guam and Hawaii. The company builds hydrant fuel systems (imagine huge gas stations for jet planes) and wharves and dry docks for submarines. Dearman travels to Hawaii every three or four months to meet with the on-site crew there. As assistant project manager, Dearman coordinates the purchasing and shipping of construction materials (stainless steel pipe, cork board, rebar, concrete, etc.). Once a week, the project team has a safety meeting conference call to discuss whether there were any accidents or close calls at the job site the week before. "Safety is a No. 1 concern," says Dearman. Strategic planning, problem-solving, and knowing how to meet deadlines and budgets are essential, and Dearman says he puts to use the accounting, finance, and math classes he took in college.

Rewards: "We're improving military bases and helping keep America safe. Plus, it's just great job security—and you can make a lot of money. In construction you really get to choose your path."

Challenges: "What's really challenging is not having the knowledge that people who have been in the construction industry for years have. I'm so eager for it now, but I know I've got to put in my time."

What You Should Know About Choosing a Career

Facts About Education and Careers in the United States

- The unemployment rate in 2006 for people with less than a high school diploma was 6.8 percent compared to 2.3 percent for those with a bachelor's degree.
- Between 2003 and 2004 and 2016 and 2017, the number of public high school graduates is projected to increase 15 percent in the South, 12 percent in the West, and l percent in the Northeast; the figure is projected to decrease 4 percent in the Midwest.
- Of the 1,439,000 bachelor's degrees conferred in the United States in 2004–2005, the largest numbers of degrees were conferred in the fields of business (312,000), social sciences and history (157,000), and education (105,000).
- At the master's degree level, the largest numbers of degrees in the United States in 2004–2005 were in the fields of education (167,000) and business (143,000).
- At the doctorate level, the fields with the largest number of degrees conferred in the United States in 2004–2005 were education (7,700), engineering (6,500), health professions and related clinical sciences (5,900), biological and biomedical sciences (5,600), and psychology (5,100).
- During the period between 1980 and 2005, the earnings of those with only a high school diploma decreased by $5,600,

while the earnings of those with a bachelor's or higher degree increased by $2,300.

- Research suggests that between 50 percent and 70 percent of all college students will change their declared majors at least once.
- New college graduates are often in their first job for a period as short as one or two years.
- At least 50 percent of jobs are found through networking. Research shows that fewer than 20 percent of jobs are listed in the classifieds.
- Careers in the farming, fishing, and forestry industries are projected to decline by 3 percent between 2006 and 2016.
- Careers in production are projected to decline by 5 percent between 2006 and 2016.
- A 53 percent growth in positions for network systems and data communications analysts is projected between 2006 and 2016.

Facts About Education and Careers in Canada

- The average hourly income in Canada in 2004 was $18.07.
- The average earnings for someone working in the trades in Canada is $39,000 per year. Of these, careers in creative and design arts were the lowest, with an average annual salary of $16,463; civil engineering technologies were the highest with an average annual salary of $40,570.
- In Canada the average annual salary for someone with a bachelor's degree was $50,000. The lowest-paid areas were music and applied arts, with salaries just over $23,000 annually. The highest-paid area was dentistry, with an annual salary of $91,790.
- The Canadian government expects that one million new jobs will be created by 2012, with job growth fastest in health, natural and applied sciences, the arts, culture, recreation, and sport.
- In Canada, the average person with a high school diploma will start a career earning $17,000 per year at the age of seventeen. At age sixty that person will be earning less than $40,000 per

year. A person with a bachelor's degree will enter the labor force at around age twenty-one at $30,000 per year and will be earning $75,000 per year at age sixty.

- On average in Canada, 5 percent of workers are unemployed. In occupations that most often require a university degree, the rate is 2.6 percent; for those that require a college or trade diploma, 4.2 percent; for those requiring less than a high school diploma, the rate climbs to 9.6 percent.
- In Canada, 72.5 percent of people aged fifteen to sixty-four were employed in 2005, compared to 67.5 percent in 1995.

Facts About Education and Careers Around the World

- China has twice as many university graduates as the United States, which used to be the world leader.
- Overall, children in nineteen World Education Indicators (WEI) countries (Argentina, Brazil, Chile, China, Egypt, India, Indonesia, Jamaica, Jordan, Malaysia, Paraguay, Peru, Philippines, the Russian Federation, Sri Lanka, Thailand, Tunisia, Uruguay, and Zimbabwe) can expect to spend about fourteen years in school, about four years less than in an average Organisation for Economic Co-operation and Development (OECD) country (Austria, Belgium, Canada, Denmark, Finland, France, Germany, Holland, Italy, Japan, Norway, Sweden, United Kingdom, United States, and West Germany). The gap is largely explained by lower WEI participation rates in upper secondary and postsecondary education.
- Most of the WEI country participants are close to achieving universal primary education.
- In an average WEI country, just more than one in five upper secondary students is enrolled in technical and vocational education, which is about one-half of the OECD average.
- In most WEI countries, more than one-third of the population aged twenty-five to sixty-four has completed at least upper secondary schooling, compared to more than two-thirds, on average, in OECD countries.

- Brazil has made one of the most dramatic improvements in the levels of primary education attained, moving from 40 percent in 1960 to 76 percent in 1980, and finally 90 percent in 2005 for teens aged fifteen to seventeen.
- The fastest growth in high school education has been recorded in Malaysia, where the proportion of people with an upper secondary education increased from 30 percent for forty-five- to fifty-four-year-olds to 73 percent for twenty- to twenty-four-year-olds by 2004.
- Between 1992 and 2005, Brazil, Czech Republic, Germany, Hungary, Japan, Poland, Slovac Republic, Sweden, Switzerland, and Turkey all experienced an annual growth rate loss in employment between –1.2 percent and 0 percent. Ireland had the highest employment growth rate with an increase of 2.2 percent, followed by Spain (1.8 percent) and New Zealand (1 percent).
- Iceland had the highest rate of employment for people aged fifteen to sixty-four in 2005, with a rate of 84.4 percent, followed by 77.2 percent in Switzerland, 75.5 percent in Denmark, and 74.6 percent in New Zealand. The United States ranked ninth with 71.5percent.
- Employment rates for men decreased in eighteen countries between 1992 and 2005, with an annual fall of more than 0.5 percent in Germany, Poland, and Turkey. For women, on the other hand, employment rates grew in twenty-five countries with increases of 1.5 percent per year or more recorded for Belgium, Greece, Ireland, Italy, Netherlands, and Spain.
- Many countries in the world have a required military service for boys leaving school. These include: Albania, Armenia, Austria, Belarus, Brazil, Chile, China (exists in theory but is not enforced), Colombia, Denmark, Egypt (may be delayed to twenty-eight years of age for education), Finland, Germany, Greece, Iran, Israel, South Korea, Mexico, Norway, Poland, Russia, Serbia, Singapore, Sweden, Switzerland, Taiwan, Turkey, and Ukraine.

What You Should Do About Choosing a Career

Fiachra O'Sullivan, vice president of Comcourse (a provider of online education services to colleges and educational organizations), was quoted by *Technology News* on April 18, 2006, as saying, "A [high school] diploma alone means an average of $717 more per month for an average worker . . . a diploma results in approximately $350,000 in increased lifetime earnings, on average."

Students drop out of high school for many reasons, but the main reason they return to school for that diploma is to improve their ability to choose a more meaningful, better-paying career. However, by the time they make the decision to return to school, many already have family responsibilities, commitments, and debts that increase the difficulty of being successful in their studies. Planning a career path should begin early, and education plays a significant role in having a successful career.

Begin Making Career Choices Before High School

Deciding on a career is all about exploring what you like to do. Get involved in a variety of school programs by the time you reach middle school or junior high, choosing from a variety of options, including drama, sports, or clubs such as yearbook or the school newspaper. These types of activities help you find out what you enjoy most. In addition, they help you develop valuable skills in working with others and gaining leadership experience.

You could also explore opportunities for teens outside of school, many of which may involve minimal expense, such as the Boy Scouts or Girl Scouts or local church organizations. Becoming involved with service groups helps you gain interpersonal skills and provides you with valuable experiences in helping others around the world. Today's economy is global, so knowledge of other cultures is important in career preparation.

Computer skills are also important in the global age, so it is important for you to become comfortable with technology. Even if your family does not have Internet access at home, you can look for computer clubs at school or community centers, or you can visit the local library. Individuals in successful careers are life-long learners, so the more comfortable you are using all services of the library, the easier it will be for you to succeed when you move on to the workplace.

High School Is the Time for Discovery

High school is a time for new independence for teens, so it is often tempting to think about having fun in the present and leaving the future to take care of itself. However, by taking careful stock of what you like to do and choosing a career plan, it is possible to combine all the great activities you enjoy with your goals for the future.

Rather than applying for that part-time job serving fast-food hamburgers with your friends, start thinking about the career you might enjoy in the future. Look for job shadowing opportunities, accompanying for a brief period of time a person who works in a field that interests you. Seek after-school or summer jobs that provide valuable work experience. Sometimes a hobby or interest can lead to a career, so it is always wise to make an inventory of your skills and look around at the community to see where those skills could be used when you have time for more after-school activities.

High school is also a period when academics are extremely important. Striving for good grades in an academic courseload will leave every door open when it comes time for college. Remember that the eleventh grade is the most important year of high school, since the grades and course selection from that year are reviewed by colleges for scholarships and admissions. You should put in the extra effort to keep your grades as high as possible. Prepare adequately for standardized tests as well: taking the PSAT/PLAN will give you a feel for how to approach the SAT/

ACT tests. High scores can make a big difference in the types and number of colleges that are open to you.

Changing Course

Just because you start out with a specific career choice in junior high school does not mean the plan cannot change when you are in high school or college. You should continue to make an honest assessment of your interests, skills, and abilities. If you start out dreaming of being an astronaut but you just cannot raise your SAT scores high enough to get into an appropriate degree program, you will need to go in a new direction.

When choices and plans need to change, then you need to explore other options. What exactly drew you to the exploration of outer space? The thrill of learning about new places? An interest in the stars and astronomy? An aptitude for mechanics and machines? Great skills with computers? Following in family tradition?

Once you examine your dreams carefully, you will be in a position to make alternative choices that really suit you. There are many ways, for example, to be a modern-day explorer or world traveler, even if it is not in outer space: travel writing, military service, working in sales for a global company, even driving a truck. The key to choosing a career is for you to know yourself, set achievable goals, and work toward them, beginning today.

American Association of Community Colleges (AACC)
AACC Guest Comments
One Dupont Circle NW, Ste. 410, Washington, DC 20036
Web site: www.aacc.nche.edu

In service since 1920, the AACC represents and advocates for more than 1,200 associate-degree granting institutions enrolling more than 12 million students—almost half of all U.S. undergraduates. AACC is the major publisher of books, monographs, and periodicals focused on community college events and issues. AACC publishes the *Community College Times* newspaper, the *Community College Journal*, and other publications.

America's Career Resource Network (ACRN)
National Training Support Center
1800 K St., Ste. 710, Washington, DC 20006
(202) 496-5577
e-mail: ntsc@dtihq.com
Web site: www.acrnetwork.org

ACRN consists of state and federal organizations that provide information, resources, and training on career and education exploration. ACRN helps people identify their skills and interests and plan an education and training course that makes the most of their natural abilities and leads directly to fulfilling work. Each month, the National Training Support Center publishes *Education and Career Connections*, a newsletter for career development professionals with the latest news and information from the field.

Mapping Your Future
Web site: www.mapping-your-future.org

Mapping Your Future is a national collaborative, public-service organization of the financial aid industry, bringing together the

expertise of the industry to provide free college, career, financial aid, and financial literacy services to students, families, and
schools.

National Center for Education Statistics (NCES)
1990 K St. NW, Washington, DC 20006
(202) 502-7300
Web site: http://nces.ed.gov

The NCES, located within the U.S. Department of Education and
the Institute of Education Sciences, is the primary federal entity
for collecting and analyzing data related to education. The NCES
provides numerous types of publications, including annual reports
such as *The Condition of Education*, which summarizes developments and trends in education using the latest available data.

**National Center on Secondary Education and Transition
(NCSET)**
6 Pattee Hall, 150 Pillsbury Dr. SE, Minneapolis, MN 55455
(612) 624-2097
fax: (612) 624-9344
e-mail: ncset@umn.edu
Web site: www.ncset.org

The NCSET coordinates national resources, offers technical assistance, and disseminates information related to secondary education and transition for youth with disabilities
in order to create opportunities for young people to achieve
successful futures. The NCSET Web site offers various publications, including *Parent Briefs*, which promote effective parent involvement in secondary education and transition, and
Information Briefs, which address trends and developments in
secondary education and transition.

**National Dissemination Center for Children with Disabilities
(NICHCY)**
PO Box 1492, Washington, DC 20013
(800) 695-0285

fax: (202) 884-8441
Web site: www.nichcy.org

The NICHCY serves the United States as a central source of information on: disabilities in infants, toddlers, children, and youth; IDEA, which is the law authorizing special education; No Child Left Behind (as it relates to children with disabilities); and research-based information on effective educational practices. The NICHCY produces several different publications, including *News Digest*, a series that takes an in-depth look at current disability issues such as parent concerns, legal issues, and educational rights of children with disabilities.

National Education Association (NEA)
1201 Sixteenth St. NW, Washington, DC 20036-3290
(202) 833-4000
fax: (202) 822-7974
Web site: www.nea.org

The NEA is a 3.2-million-member organization working to improve schools across the nation, decrease the high school dropout rate, and ensure that every child has a good education. The NEA publishes reports, state and national education statistics, school funding data, and *NEA in the News*, a weekly roundup of major education news stories. In addition, the NEA Professional Library is on the Web site, where visitors can purchase various products and sign up for the *NEA Professional Library Newsletter*.

National Institute for Literacy
1775 I St. NW, Ste. 730, Washington, DC 20006-2401
(202) 233-2025
fax: (202) 233-2050
Web site: www.nifl.gov

The National Institute for Literacy, a federal agency, provides leadership on literacy issues, including the improvement of reading instruction for children, youth, and adults. The National Institute for Literacy produces the newsletter *QEd: Scientific*

Evidence for Adult Literacy Educators, in addition to developing publications for both families and educators.

National Research Center for Career and Technical Education (NRCCTE)
University of Louisville
331 Education Bldg., Louisville, KY 40292
(502) 852-0639
fax: (707) 539-2710
Web site: www.nccte.org

The NRCCTE is the primary agent for generating scientifically based knowledge, dissemination, professional development, and technical assistance to improve career and technical education in the United States. The NRCCTE's Web site offers various publications, including *In Brief: Fast Facts for Policy and Practice*.

Office of Postsecondary Education (OPE)
U.S. Department of Education
Office of Postsecondary Education
1990 K St. NW, Washington, DC 20006
(202) 502-7750
Web site: www.ed.gov/ope

The OPE formulates federal postsecondary education policy and administers programs that address critical national needs in support of their mission to increase access to quality postsecondary education. The OPE's Web site provides news briefs, policy documents and initiatives, and reports such as *The Secretary's Fifth Annual Report on Teacher Quality: A Highly Qualified Teacher in Every Classroom*.

United States Distance Learning Association (USDLA)
8 Winter St., Ste. 508, Boston, MA 02108
(800) 275-5162
fax: (617) 399-1771
Web site: www.usdla.org

The USDLA provides national leadership in the field of distance learning. It also serves as a catalyst for the formation of partnerships among education, business, health care, and government. The USDLA Distance Learning Link Program (DLLP) is a showcase of distance learning institutions offering degrees, certificates, and courses in distance education and training. There are course offerings for the bachelor, master, and doctoral degree programs as well as noncredit courses for adult learners and others who wish to pursue a specific skill or interest. The USDLA's publications include *Distance Learning—A Magazine for Leaders* and *Electronic Learning Communities: Issues and Practices*.

Julia K. Boehm and Sonja Lyubomirsky, "Does Happiness Promote Career Success?" *Journal of Career Assessment*, February 2008.

Sean Cavanagh, "Citizen Schools: An After-Hours Adventure—Professionals Mentoring Middle-Grades Students," *Education Week*, January 2007.

Peter A. Creed, Wendy Patton, and Lee-Ann Prideaux, "Predicting Change over Time in Career Planning and Career Exploration for High School Students," *Journal of Adolescence*, June 2007.

Alisha Hyslop, "Establish Postsecondary Preparation and Expectations for All," *Techniques: Connecting Education and Careers*, September 2007.

Petri Koivisto, Jukka Vuori, and Elina Nykyri, "Effects of the School-to-Work Group Method Among Young People," *Journal of Vocational Behavior*, April 2007.

Lydia Lum, "Community Colleges Are Portals to New Career Paths," *Diverse: Issues in Higher Education*, November 2007.

Principal Leadership, "A Grand Entrance to Higher Education: Personalization Is Key to Encouraging Students to Go to College," November 2007.

Susan Reese, "A Message That Matters," *Techniques: Connecting Education and Careers*, February 2007.

Alison Taylor and Bonnie Watt-Malcolm, "Expansive Learning Through High School Apprenticeship: Opportunities and Limits," *Journal of Education and Work*, February 2007.

Kathleen Vale, "Technology Drives Career and Technical Education in High School Reform," *Education Digest*, April 2007.

Julie Miller Vick and Jennifer S. Furlong, "Use Your Summer Wisely," *Chronicle of Higher Education*, July 2007.

Gene White, Douglas Lare, Suzanne Mueller, Patricia Smeaton, and Faith Waters, "The Virtual Education Academy: A Novel Approach to Engaging At-Risk Students," *Kappa Delta Pi Record*, Fall 2007.

PICTURE CREDITS

Image copyright aceshot1, 2008. Used under license from
Shutterstock.com, 36

AP Images, 22, 28, 42, 53, 87

© Michael Doolittle/Alamy, 92

Image copyright Andrew Gentry, 2008. Used under license
from Shutterstock.com, 9

© Dennis MacDonald/Alamy, 13

Robert Nickelsberg/Getty Images, 17

Image copyright PhotoCreate, 2008. Used under license from
Shutterstock.com, 8

Image copyright Emil Pozar, 2008. Used under license from
Shutterstock.com, 65

© Stock Connection Blue/Alamy, 59

Image copyright Nicholas Sutcliffe, 2008. Used under license
from Shutterstock.com, 84

Steve Zmina, 14, 24, 29, 34, 41, 51, 61, 68, 78, 95